"Another provocative . . . work from a playwright who has become a leading chronicler of urban angst . . . The playwright's gift for pungent, earthy dialogue is on display throughout . . . *The Little Flower of East Orange* eventually gets under your skin in a way that tidier dramas don't often manage."

—FRANK SCHECK, *New York Post*

"Searing . . . Guirgis has never had a problem locating pain's funny bone . . . *The Little Flower of East Orange* . . . blooms defiantly, and ultimately cheeringly, through the cracks in the city sidewalk." —BOB KENDT, *Newsday*

"I'm content to keep following Guirgis wherever his wayward talent leads him." —JEREMY MCCARTER, *New York*

"Intense . . . Guirgis . . . is known for colorful characters and raw, street-smart language. He's true to form and shows great sensitivity, too . . . After *Little Flower*, you'll either want to call your mother or regret that you can't."

—JOE DZIEMIANOWICZ, New York *Daily News*

"A play that's imperfect and raw but also deeply felt and at times startling in its bruising intimacy . . . Guirgis is a playwright of too singular gifts to pen the hackneyed, heart-tugging drama of reconciliation and closure [that the play's] description might imply. His rough-edged work has a distinctive voice, full of profane, jagged poetry, prickly humor, grimy lyricism and anguish not easily quelled." —DAVID ROONEY, *Variety*

STEPHEN ADLY GUIRGIS

THE LITTLE FLOWER
OF EAST ORANGE

Stephen Adly Guirgis has been a member of New York City's LAByrinth Theater Company since 1994. His plays have been produced on five continents and throughout the United States. The premiere of *The Little Flower of East Orange*, starring Ellen Burstyn and directed by Philip Seymour Hoffman, played to an extended run at the Public Theater. His other plays include *Our Lady of 121st Street*, which was included as one of the ten best plays of 2003 in *The Best Plays Theater Yearbook*, the annual chronicle of U.S. theater, and received Best Play nominations from the Lucille Lortel Foundation, the Drama Desk, and the Outer Critics Circle; *Jesus Hopped* the *"A" Train*, which won the Edinburgh Fringe First Award, was named a Detroit Free Press Best Play of the Year, and received the Barrymore Award and a Laurence Olivier Award nomination as London's best new play; *In Arabia, We'd All Be Kings*, which was named one of the best productions of 2007 by the Los Angeles Drama Critics Circle; and *The Last Days of Judas Iscariot*. In 2008, *Judas* had its European premiere in a critically acclaimed production at London's Almeida Theater under the direction of the Headlong Theater's Rupert Goold. All five plays were originally produced by LAByrinth, directed by Philip Seymour Hoffman, and published for the trade by Faber and Faber, Inc., and in acting editions by Dramatists Play Service. Guirgis's one-act play *Dominica: The Fat Ugly 'Ho* was directed by Adam Rapp as part of the 2006 EST Marathon. His television writing credits include scripts for *NYPD Blue*, *The Sopranos*, David Milch's CBS drama series *Big Apple*, and Shane Salerno's NBC series *UC: Undercover*. He was awarded a 2006 PEN/Laura Pels Award, a 2006 Whiting Award, and a 2004 TCG Fellowship.

Guirgis attended the 2004 Sundance Screenwriters Lab and was named one of 2004's 25 New Faces of Indie Film by *Filmmaker* magazine. He is the recipient of new play commissions from Manhattan Theatre Club, L.A.'s Center Theater Group, and South Coast Repertory, and is a member of New Dramatists, the MCC Theater Playwrights' Coalition, New River Dramatists, and the Actors Studio's Playwright-Director's Unit. He developed and directed Liza Cólon-Zayas's *Sistah Supreme* for the Hip-Hop Theater Festival and Marco Greco's award-winning *Behind the Counter with Mussolini* in New York and Los Angeles.

As an actor, Guirgis appeared in Brett C. Leonard's *Guinea Pig Solo*, produced by the LAByrinth Theater Company at the Public Theater in New York, and has had leading roles in Todd Solondz's *Palindromes*, Brett C. Leonard's *Jailbait*, and Kenneth Lonergan's upcoming film *Margaret*. Other film credits include Charlie Kaufman's *Synecdoche, New York* and Adam Rapp's *Blackbird*. A former violence prevention specialist and HIV educator, he lives in New York City.

THE LITTLE FLOWER
OF EAST ORANGE

THE
LITTLE FLOWER OF
EAST ORANGE

•

STEPHEN ADLY GUIRGIS

FARRAR, STRAUS AND GIROUX

NEW YORK

Farrar, Straus and Giroux
18 West 18th Street, New York 10011

Library of Congress Cataloging-in-Publication Data
Guirgis, Stephen Adly.
    The little flower of East Orange / Stephen Adly Guirgis. — 1st ed.
    p.   cm.
    ISBN: 978-0-86547-901-2 (pbk.)
    1. Mothers and sons—Drama.   2. Family—Drama.   I. Title.
PS3607.U49 L57 2009
812'.6—dc22

                                                            2008038867

Designed by Gretchen Achilles

www.fsgbooks.com
www.twitter.com/fsgbooks • www.facebook.com/fsgbooks

P1

FOR SONIA SOLIS, JEANNE CAMPBELL,

AND JAMIE MULLINS—

REST IN PEACE

The splendor of the rose and the whiteness of the lily do not rob the little violet of its scent nor the daisy of its simple charm. I realized that if every tiny flower wanted to be a rose, spring would lose its loveliness and there would be no wildflowers to make the meadows gay.

—SAINT THÉRÈSE OF LISIEUX

INTRODUCTION

A couple of years ago I was kind of fucked up in the head and the heart, and so I attended a sort of spiritual/wellness retreat down South. There was a woman at the retreat who had recently lost her mother to cancer, and she was very angry and very sad and very inconsolable and alone. The other people at the retreat were empathetic toward her at first, but she kept them at a distance, and pretty quickly they kind of just let her be. I started talking with the woman, and after a day or two she started talking back and sharing her story with me, and before long she was able to join the others and become part of the group, and I remember that I felt very good about that at the time. I kind of thought to myself, "Other people didn't seem to care enough about this woman, but I did. Other people kept her at a distance, but I didn't. What a good, caring guy I must be."

Four months later, I was smoking a cigarette and freezing my ass off outside a hospice in the Bronx where my own mother was now rapidly dying of cancer, and where I was now the one who was angry and sad and inconsolable and alone, and my thoughts suddenly turned to that woman from the retreat and those other people who were there, and I realized the following: Those other people were not uncaring; they had kept their distance because they were scared of the inevitable losses in their own lives. And what I had given that woman back then was really only a well-meaning but contrived appearance of intimacy—because the truth was that I had kept my distance just like the others, because I was scared too. And in that moment outside my mom's hospice in the Bronx, I wanted to call that woman and tell her about my newfound discovery and apologize to her, until I realized that she had already been through all of this, and therefore she already knew. I mention this for two reasons: first, because I've come to learn that the world can be soberly divided into those who've lost their mothers and those who haven't; and second, because in my particular case, my mom was very much alive when I started writing this play and she was dead before I was halfway through.

The play itself came about because I was fortunate enough in 2005 to receive a commission to write a new play for a theater in midtown Manhattan. I was excited about it, because all my plays have been done below Twenty-third Street and I liked the challenge of trying to write a play that would bridge the gap between my kind of audience (younger, downtown) with their kind of audience (um, not quite so young). Now, I'm not one of those people who roll their eyes and look down their noses at the older audiences. These are, after all, the people who have kept theater alive in this city for the last fifty years, and it's not because they're idiots. In general, they care a great deal about the theater, they support it generously, and they mostly know the difference between a good play and a piece of crap. These are people who saw Laurette Taylor in *The Glass Menagerie* and Brando in *Streetcar*. They saw all the great musicals. Many of them saw the early Albee plays, and both witnessed and nurtured the birth of Off-Broadway. To my mind, these are folks who know a thing or two, and I wanted to try and write something that would speak to and challenge them as well as speak to and challenge my kind of crowd. I thought of my mom, who grew up in the $1.10 balconies of old Broadway, and I thought of my peers, and I thought of all the students still coming up. I thought of them all sitting together. And I got excited. And here was the clincher: the theater had these beautiful, plush red velvet seats. And as they took me on a tour of their space, I was, I admit, transfixed by those red velvet seats. In fact, as I sat in one of those very comfortable red velvet seats and stared out at the stage and its wings, I kinda started crying a little. I decided, right then and there, that I would write a family play. Everybody's got a family, so everybody might in some way relate to whatever it is I ended up writing. There. Done. I told the awesome Literary Manager my intentions, she said "Great," and that was that. I was pretty thrilled . . .

Of course, writing a play is easier said than done. And the process of writing this one was especially challenging—and then my mom just suddenly died. Before she died, I was kinda having a pretty rough time in general anyway, so when she became quite ill without warning and then passed away about a month later, the whole world essentially stopped. My sister and I took care of my mom every day and night until she passed, and then, the night she died, I immediately moved back in with my dad, where I still am, because he's old and his life had just gotten ripped out from under him, and I just couldn't imagine him being left all alone. So I moved in with him, and it was tough. My mom was the family's common denominator— she was the emotional linchpin, the alpha parent—and now everything just got real quiet. For quite some time. And since my play—though not strictly autobiographical—dealt with both family issues and aspects of my mom herself, I had no desire or ability to go sit back at a desk and deal with it. But eventually, after some months passed, I did. I would sneak off into the back room and try to write and nothing would happen, but at least I was sitting there. Then, one night, words started coming out, and I ended up being able to write what is now the first scene in Act Two, where the mom cross-examines the son about when he's going to get back together again with his long-gone 3500-miles-away-and-couldn't-be-happier ex-girlfriend. For other writers out there, I think it's true that some things are too fresh to write about until time has passed, and maybe that was true of me when I was writing this play, but in this particular instance, I realized later that what I had done was to take a side door back into the play. I wasn't ready to deal with the death stuff or the anger stuff, but I was able to have a little fun with the familiar reality of the overcurious and meddling mother, and the ex-girlfriend part was something I had enough distance from that I could dredge it up and see where it led.

I don't know that I've ever felt more grateful for having written anything than I felt after having written that scene that night. And then, after I wrote that scene, I was slowly able to move into more difficult territory, and eventually I had about two-thirds of a play. I called the theater with the red velvet seats, we had a reading, and the play was scheduled, but then it fell through. It fell through because of me. The play wasn't finished, and so the theater was nervous, but they still wanted to do the play—just not in the theater with red velvet seats. They wanted to do it in their other, smaller, non-red-velvet-seated space, which was more than reasonable, since the play was incomplete, but somehow, perhaps irrationally, it no longer felt right to me. People have sat on the floor during my plays—on broken seats, on milk crates, on folding metal chairs—but for some reason I just didn't want to do the play there without those red velvet seats. Stupid, I know.

Oskar Eustis at the Public Theater quickly and generously stepped in, and we ended up doing the play at the Public, where it probably should have been in the first place, and with my company, LAByrinth, as coproducers. We sold out the run and the extension, and the audiences were incredibly generous and receptive. It was interesting reading the reviews. (Why do I still read them? I dunno—'cuz I'm an idiot?) Some of the criticisms were pretty spot-on and valid, and yet I was amazed at how many reviewers just assumed that the play was my literal life story (one critic even opined, "*The Little Flower of East Orange* is proof that some lives are not worth dramatizing"). I bring this up because of something I learned during the process, which is this: I will never assume that anyone's work is purely "autobiographical" ever again, because the term is actually meaningless. We live in a world that has an insatiable need to break everything down into easily digestible bites. We are suckers for "context." I'm as guilty of that as anyone else. But any work (like a play) that requires the unconscious and the imagination and the deceptiveness of memory and emotion and feeling just isn't built to conform to our societal desire for easy context and literal truth. What we think of as "autobiographical" is nothing more than a snapshot of a sliver of a feeling associated with a real or fabricated memory felt deeply while looking out a window on a Tuesday morning. I don't think it's any more or less than just that. If you want to know something about my life, read *Jesus Hopped the "A" Train*, which is about a serial killer and a bike messenger—and I'm neither. But it will tell you just as much about what keeps me up at night as *Little Flower* does.

Lastly I gotta say that being in the theater and being able to write plays and put them on is a privilege, and pretty much a joy. The experience of writing *Little Flower* and working with Phil and the actors is one I wouldn't trade for anything. We have plans to bring *Little Flower* back, and I am going to do some rewrites and revisions. Hopefully, you can come see it, or see it again. This play is not my story, but it was written, like all the others, in the hope that it may in some small way tell your story, or rather, our story. Thanks for reading this.

THE LITTLE FLOWER
OF EAST ORANGE

The Little Flower of East Orange was first produced by the LAByrinth Theater Company at the Public Theater on April 6, 2008. It was directed by Philip Seymour Hoffman; sets were designed by Narelle Sissons; costumes by Mimi O'Donnell; lights by Japhy Weideman; and sound by David Van Tieghem. The production manager was Monica Moore. The cast was as follows:

THERESE MARIE	*Ellen Burstyn*
AUNT MARGARET/JUSTINA/NURSE 2	*Elizabeth Canavan*
MAGNOLIA/NURSE 1/POPE JOHN XXIII	*Liza Colón-Zayas*
DETECTIVE BAKER/JIMMY STEWART/ FATHER LANDER/ORDERLY	*Arthur French*
NADINE/CATHLEEN	*Gillian Jacobs*
DR. SHANKAR	*Ajay Naidu*
FRANCIS JAMES	*Howie Seago*
DANNY	*Michael Shannon*
DAVID HALZIG/PLAINCLOTHES DETECTIVE/ SURGEON 1/BOBBY KENNEDY/UNCLE BARNEY	*Sidney Williams*
ESPINOSA/SURGEON 2	*David Zayas*

CHARACTERS

THERESE MARIE: ~~In her seventies. The mother.~~

DANNY: In his thirties. The son.

JUSTINA: In her thirties. The daughter.

MAGNOLIA: In her thirties or forties. A Jamaican nurse.

DETECTIVE BAKER: In his fifties or sixties. African-American. A cop.

NADINE: In her twenties. Danny's runaway girlfriend from rehab.

DR. SHANKAR: In his thirties or forties. The attending physician and chief of staff.

FRANCIS JAMES: The grandfather. He's a ghost. He lives in memory.

DAVID HALZIG: aka *puto*. In his thirties or forties. Another parent's troubled son.

ESPINOSA: In his thirties or forties. A Dominican hospital orderly.

OTHER CHARACTERS: Plainclothes Detective, Nurse 1, Nurse 2, Surgeon 1, Surgeon 2, Jimmy Stewart, Cathleen, Bobby Kennedy, Pope John XXIII, Uncle Barney, Aunt Margaret.

SETTING

New York City. The present and the past.

ACT I

SCENE 1

A plainclothes detective in casual attire and an NYPD windbreaker uncuffs the prisoner.

DANNY Good evening . . . I'm Danny, and I'm the author and narrator of this story. I call this a story because truth is elusive, subjective, and fleeting. I also call this a story 'cuz I was high like Ned the Wino through a lot of it . . . However, I'm not trying to hide behind any of that "unreliable narrator" bullshit. No. This is me. My story. I'm not interested enough in storytelling to try and make shit up. Up at Otisville, I got a counselor named Mr. Benedek. He's a good man. One day he made the "suggestion" that me telling my story might be helpful to me. I thanked him for the suggestion, then asked if he'd sign my sheet so I could go to the yard. That's when he broke it to me that what he was asking wasn't a suggestion. So here I am . . . One more thing: some very few of you out there may know me as a writer. I'm not a writer. The only reason I wrote a book was because someone told me once, "You should write a book," so I did, and then I felt a little less like a loser, and people paid a little more attention to me, like, cooler people and girls— and then the IRS . . . People should be strong enough to be who they really want to be—not what the world or their family thinks they should be. Which brings me to why I'm here . . . (*Clears his throat*) Once upon a time, there was a little girl who could roller-skate over rooftops . . .

MAGNOLIA *and* ESPINOSA *enter hurriedly with an old woman, unconscious on a gurney. It is very dark and very late. Trailing behind them is a ghost named* FRANCIS JAMES *who hovers throughout and from a distance. They take no notice of him. The old woman*—THERESE MARIE—*is hooked up to an IV, and wears an oxygen mask and a cervical collar around her neck. There are two beds in the room. One is occupied, but curtained off. The other is empty.* ESPINOSA *and* MAGNOLIA *are preparing to transfer the old woman to the empty bed.*

ESPINOSA (*midstream*) I'm tellin' you, Magnolia—that ol' bitch in 11A—

MAGNOLIA Miss Nathanson?

ESPINOSA I swear ta God—I'm gonna get me a santera to put a spell on that ol' bitch, make her drop dead from a fuckin' coronary like she shoulda done ten years ago!

MAGNOLIA You evil, Mr. Espinosa.

ESPINOSA Yo, I ain't the one that's evil! That ol' *bruja*— know what she is?—she's the face of the diabolical—das what she is! She a cotton-ball bitch!

MAGNOLIA Oh, I see. 'Cuz she report you for smoking, right?

ESPINOSA Das right. "'Cuz she report me for smoking"!! C'mon now: bitch is 159 years old, dyin' of, like, eighty-seven debilitating illnesses, she's gotta be worried about a little fuckin' secondhand *smoke*?? After all I do for that no-toof bitch?

STEPHEN ADLY GUIRGIS

MAGNOLIA (*with a nod*) Okay, quiet now.

ESPINOSA For what?

MAGNOLIA (*re: the patient behind the curtain*) Miss Halzig.

ESPINOSA Miss Halzig?! That bitch couldn't hear a hydrogen bomb go off if they blew that shit off the top of her forehead! She don't even know her own name! Watch! (*Pulls back the curtain to* MISS HALZIG'S *bed.*) (*to* MISS HALZIG) *BOO!! GODZILLA!! OSAMA BIN LADEN!!* (to MAGNOLIA) You see?

MAGNOLIA That's not funny.

ESPINOSA Then why you laughin'?

MAGNOLIA I'm laughin' at a fool, Mr. Espinosa.

ESPINOSA Is that right?

MAGNOLIA Dat's right. Laughin' at a Puerto Rican fool gonna lose his job.

ESPINOSA *Dominicano, mami!* No Puerto Rico! *Dominicano!* And yeah: for eight-fifty an hour and no benefits, they can take this job, stick it in a fuckin' catheter, and pump that shit up they peeholes all I fuckin' care! All them mothahfuckahs! Nurses. Doctors. This lady right here! Sixteen hours straight, four a.m., and I *still* got a pepperoni pizza in my locker I ain't eaten 'cuz EMS had to roll in with this mystery bitch! . . .

DANNY . . . Last spring, on the night my mother disappeared, I was in a drug rehab in Scottsdale, Arizona, dropping a half dozen hits of acid and smoking uncut rock with a buxom young Republican state senator's daughter from Butte, Montana, named Nadine Powers. Nadine had snuck into my room, and we were pretending we were the last two survivors on earth, and it was our mission to repopulate all species of man, beast, and bird:

NADINE (*nearing intense orgasm*) Oh God, Danny! Fuck me like an ostrich, Danny! Bury your head in my sand!—

DANNY (*approaching nirvana*)—I'm an ostrich, Nadine! I have feathers and they're flapping! I'm a pumping, pluming ostrich!—"NeeYeet!" "NeeYeet!!"

NADINE (*virtually vibrating*) "Wabeeeechu! Wabeeeeeechu!" Oh, Danny—(terrariums, Johnny Depp, the boys who raped me)—kiss me with lollipops, Danny! Flap me, peck me, ride me south!

DANNY (*a towering inferno*) Oh, Nadine, I wanna fuck you now like a lovely but fierce llama from an ancient and sacred South American nation, Nadine!

NADINE (*as a llama*) Baaa!

DANNY Baaa!

NADINE (*an imminent tidal wave*) You have pretty eyes, Llama Lover Man—

DANNY (*ecstatically transforming*) Baaa—

NADINE (*the earth shaking*)—like a pretty cartoon cat from cartoons on the cartoon channel! Like cinnamon toast with sugar and compassion and Technicolor with all love and no commercials!

DANNY (*the heavens aligning*) You're the only one who understands me, Nadine!

NADINE I wanna fuck you on the floor of the Montana state senate, Danny!

DANNY (*to audience*) And then the phone rang—"Hello?"

JUSTINA (*a ferocious hysterical tsunami*): Shriek!, shriek!, sob, sob! *DANNY!*/Shriek, shriek!, wail, wail! *MOMMY GONE!!*/Howl, howl, sedative, sedative, *get on a fuckin' plane selfish addict fuck!*/Hysteria, hysteria, gasp, moan, cry, *asthma onset—your fuckin' fault!!* Sniffle, sniffle, passive-aggressive silence—*the world is fucking ending*/ Sniffle, sniffle, Valium, Seconal, *airport now!*/Moan, moan, audible gasp. *At work. Can't talk. I do everything. Ready to slit my throat with carving knife.*/Cry, cry, bellow, bellow *MOMMY GONE MOMMY GONE MOMMY GONE. I hate you!* Cry cry wail! Wail— indecipherable threats—*JetBlue motherfucker—book that shit!*—slam. Click. Dial tone.

DANNY, *dazed*.

NADINE . . . Who was that?
DANNY I think the world is ending.
NADINE I'll get my things.

The lights cross-fade back to the hospital room.

DR. SHANKAR Is this the Jane Doe, Esther?
MAGNOLIA Yes, Doctor. The police, they took a fingerprint, she don't have no wallet, no identification, nothing. She got a plastic bag with some small articles there.
ESPINOSA All she got in there is some mints, a book of crossword puzzles, and some Chessmen cookies.
DR. SHANKAR Vitals?

MAGNOLIA Body temperature indicates hypothermia; electrolyte disturbances in the blood, very low oxygen levels, and she has substantial instability in her back and neck. EMS say she sustain a fall, Doctor, down the stairs in her wheelchair at the Cloisters—

DR. SHANKAR Cloisters?! Call Columbia Presbyterian, have them pick her up.

MAGNOLIA EMS reroute her from them to us 'cuz they got heavy intake in the ER over there—Project Fire, something, they said.

DR. SHANKAR Right, like we're so overstaffed and under-emergencied. Okay, I'll run an antibiotic stat. Let's see if we can get an ID by morning.

MAGNOLIA Doctor, she not conscious now, but she was moving and shifting before and she was speakin' crazy like she have a lot of pain. Grave pain, Doctor. She need a morphine drip, I think.

DR. SHANKAR We don't want medication masking consciousness. Give her some liquid Tylenol and keep me apprised.

DR. SHANKAR *begins exiting.*

MAGNOLIA Doctor, this lady need morphine, Doctor.

DR. SHANKAR Esther, do you have something in writing that tells me this woman isn't *allergic* to morphine? Or that any morphine we give her won't induce respiratory arrest?

MAGNOLIA Allergy to morphine—that's very rare, I think.

DR. SHANKAR Yes. And so are Jane Does with no medical

histories to draw from. Do you remember the patient in
13B last year?

MAGNOLIA Yes. But if this patient here, she expire from shock
because she was not adequately sedated, Doctor?

DR. SHANKAR Then she expires. Let's hope she doesn't.
(*Beat.*) Good night, Esther. Espinosa.

ESPINOSA She ain't Esther, Doc. She Magnolia.

DR. SHANKAR . . . Yes, of course you are—it's just—you and
Esther—anyway—

ESPINOSA Esther's four times her size, Doc. Put her in a
diaper and slick her hair back, she could wrestle sumo.

DR. SHANKAR Uh . . . Yes.

ESPINOSA They look nothing alike.

DR. SHANKAR In any case—

ESPINOSA —Now, Doc: we was here when this patient
arrived. Now, I ain't got no diplomas hangin', you know,
by the fireplace—

DR. SHANKAR —Espinosa, there's a bedpan in 11A. Tend
to it.

ESPINOSA I'm just saying.

DR. SHANKAR Bedpan.

ESPINOSA Fine. (*under his breath*) Fuckin' Papa Smurf . . .

DR. SHANKAR Yes, I am Papa Smurf—and you are Clean Up
Bedpans Smurf, okay, my friend?

ESPINOSA (*under breath*) Ma-mow. (*Exits.*)

DR. SHANKAR Now, look: you're a good nurse, that's very
evident—

MAGNOLIA Doctor—

DR. SHANKAR This woman is unconscious. Her vitals are
fading despite our best efforts to stabilize her. Should

she revive, I will address the patient's pain management situation at that time and with her consent and not a minute before. Do you remember Mr. Jenkins? Wandered off to the roof, got himself locked out, and froze to death? The man never had a visitor in months—but I still have a ten-million-dollar negligence suit on behalf of the family on my desk.

MAGNOLIA Yes, Doctor.

DR. SHANKAR This woman doesn't need morphine—she needs a priest. Liquid Tylenol. Nothing more.

MAGNOLIA Yes, Doctor.

DR. SHANKAR Very good then. Carry on, Mongolia.

The doctor exits.

THERESE MARIE *stirs slightly, then fades again.*

MAGNOLIA *turns down the lights and sits by the old woman's bedside, holding her hand.*

DANNY Magnolia Jarvis kept my mother alive that night.

MAGNOLIA I didn't do nuthin' special.

DANNY You held her hand.

MAGNOLIA 'Cuz I liked her face.

DANNY You were there when she woke up.

MAGNOLIA Christian charity.

DANNY You didn't take offense when she mistook you for Jackie Robinson:

THERESE MARIE (*to* MAGNOLIA) . . . Jackie Robinson? Oh, my! Is that you?

MAGNOLIA I am Magnolia, miss, you're in a hospital—

THERESE MARIE Oh, I was just over the moon for you, Jackie—OVER THE MOON—you know, "loopy"?—listening to your games on the radio! Stealing those bases!

MAGNOLIA Let me dry your eye.

THERESE MARIE Oh, I'm ashamed I'm crying, but you lifted me, Jackie. Lifted! And when that Dixie Walker tried to make the Dodgers go on strike until the owners removed you—God help me—I heard Dixie on the radio and I shouted, I shouted right at the radio, "Go to hell, Dixie Walker, you redneck so-and-so, who in the hell needs you anyway?" Oh, that sonuvabitch!

MAGNOLIA Rest now.

THERESE MARIE Do you see Pee Wee Reese much, Jackie? Oh, I adored him! Adored him. A little fireplug, no bigger than a table lamp, but he had fire! Oh, I loved that little Pee Wee! Do you see him much, Jackie? Do you?

MAGNOLIA . . . Sometimes, yes.

THERESE MARIE Oh, that's nice. He stood up for you, that little gnat of a man, didn't he?

MAGNOLIA What's your name, miss?

THERESE MARIE . . . Oh, Jackie, I'm sorry, but I'm in an awful lot of pain right now.

MAGNOLIA Won't you just tell me your name? I could sign a football for you?

THERESE MARIE Football? Jackie, don't be silly, you played baseball.

MAGNOLIA Yes. Baseball. Would you like a little water?

THERESE MARIE Oh yes, please.

MAGNOLIA *holds the cup.* THERESE *drinks.*

THERESE MARIE Is there anything you can give me for pain?

MAGNOLIA You have a drip going into your arm. See?

THERESE MARIE I'm sorry.

MAGNOLIA Sorry for what?

THERESE MARIE I'm sorry . . .

MAGNOLIA Rest now. Okay? You rest.

The ghost, FRANCIS JAMES, *appears to* THERESE MARIE.

THERESE MARIE Poppa?

MAGNOLIA What, miss?

FRANCIS JAMES *speaks sign language to her. His signs are emphatic. He also speaks with his voice, but since he's deaf, his voice is low and guttural.*

FRANCIS JAMES You are not the boss of this house! You are not the boss of this house! Now pick it up and throw it all out! All of it!

THERESE MARIE *signs back and speaks.*

THERESE MARIE But, Poppa—

MAGNOLIA What you doing, miss?

THERESE MARIE (*to* MAGNOLIA) My father. My father. (*to Poppa, signing and speaking*) I'm—sorry—Poppa. I'm—sorry.

MAGNOLIA Sorry for what?

THERESE MARIE The pictures on the table. He doesn't understand about Tyrone Power. (*reacting to her father's blows*) Oh! Oh! Oh!

MAGNOLIA What's the matter, miss?

THERESE MARIE Oh. Oh. He doesn't mean it . . . Oh . . . He's a good, decent man . . .

MAGNOLIA Yes he is.

FRANCIS JAMES *disappears.*

THERESE MARIE A fine man, a decent man.

MAGNOLIA Yes.

THERESE MARIE From the pope, a handsome plaque, my poppa. My books . . .

MAGNOLIA Yes.

THERESE MARIE (*nodding out*) . . . I'm ready. Father Lander, the textbooks . . . Ready . . . Tell Poppa . . . (*Drifts off.*)

DANNY And then—my mother flatlined.

We see circus lights and hear sirens, and sounds vaguely reminiscent of a street fair or carnival. Doctors and nurses descend upon the dying woman with screens and contraptions and surgical clip lights. FRANCIS JAMES *looks on as we hear the medical team's harried voices:*

NURSE 1 Blood glucose. Infected wounds. Heart monitor—stat!

SURGEON 2 Morphine pump's not encoded. Smashed coccyx—stat!

NURSE 2 Sewed bones, grafted bones, sewn together, ripped apart. She's fading again! . . .

DANNY My grandfather Francis James was loved by many and admired by all. My grandfather went hungry so his children could eat. My grandfather was an alcoholic who suffered from occasional outbursts of temper.

The lights continue to blare and whirl, and the doctors continue at a frenzied pace, and the sounds of hospital hardware mixes with those of organ grinders and carousels and Irish saloon singers playing out-of-tune pianos.

SURGEON 1 Depression. Stat!

NURSE 1 Probable concussion. Stat!

SURGEON 2 Head smashed into the boiler. Stat!

NURSE 2 A good decent man. Stat!

DANNY One violent, chaotic night, when my mother was nine years old, she made the decision that someone had to protect her mother and her little sister.

We now see the backlit vague impression of an old tenement building—and in the shadows of the tenement we see and hear a young girl's screams, and a deaf woman's cries, and the dull thud of a nine-year-old head being repeatedly smashed into a boiler.

NURSE 1 Locked in the basement! Stat!

SURGEON 1 More oxygen! Stat!

NURSE 2 Asphyxiation! Stat!

SURGEON 2 He can't hear you! Stat!

DANNY My mom confronted my grandfather and made him a *promise*. She promised him that if he ever touched her mother or her sister again that she would be awfully sorry, but she would have to fetch the police and telephone Uncle Barney immediately.

THERESE MARIE Poppa!

SURGEON 1 Waves of pain! Stat!

NURSE 2 "Can't take the heat, get outta the kitchen!" Stat!

SURGEON 1 Secret garden! Stat!

NURSE 1 Momma just stood by. Stat!

DANNY And so from that day on, Francis James never touched her sister or her mother again.

THERESE MARIE Poppa!

SURGEON 2 We're losing her!

DANNY Instead, he would only beat her.

THERESE MARIE *is suddenly upright and conscious and weeping like a terrified child. The chaos continues around her.*

And then a handsome black man in a World War II air force uniform enters amid the tumult. And though chaos remains onstage, he is suddenly all we can really see and hear.

JIMMY STEWART (*singing*)
You're nobody till somebody loves you.

THERESE MARIE I know you!

JIMMY STEWART
You're nobody till somebody cares.

They dance. Music, replacing JIMMY STEWART*'s vocals. A series of spins, as—*

THERESE MARIE . . . I used to roller-skate over rooftops!

JIMMY STEWART I bet you did!

THERESE MARIE I know you, don't I?

JIMMY STEWART (*playfully*) Well, I don't know. Do you?

THERESE MARIE Oh, I'd know you anywhere—you're—you're Jimmy Stewart, aren't you?

JIMMY STEWART Well, I suppose I am—skinny legs and all.

THERESE MARIE But Jimmy, you look different somehow.

JIMMY STEWART Do I? How?

THERESE MARIE I'm sorry. I'm confused, Jimmy. I'm in an awful lot of pain.

JIMMY STEWART I understand.

THERESE MARIE Can I tell you something, Jimmy? I know you're too old for me and I'm not pretty like those glamour gals in Hollywood, but—

Downstage, a young girl with pigtails and pajamas plays with paper dolls and sings.

CATHLEEN (*singing*)
  Button up your overcoat,
  When the wind is free.

THERESE MARIE *notices the girl, stops dancing.*

THERESE MARIE Hey! Jimmy, look! That's my sister! That's Cathleen! (*calling to her*) Oh, Cathleen! Cathleen!

You shouldn't be outside without a coat on, you'll catch cold!

JIMMY STEWART She's okay. Playing with her paper dolls. See?

CATHLEEN

Keep away from bootleg hooch
When you're on a spree.

JIMMY STEWART And Teresa—everything you did for her? She knows.

THERESE MARIE Oh, I didn't do anything.

JIMMY STEWART Who do you think put her *outside* the house that night, Teresa?

THERESE MARIE Oh . . .

JIMMY STEWART Teresa, I'm leaving now to join the Eighth Air Force—I'm gonna pilot a B-24 Liberator over Europe, if you can believe that.

THERESE MARIE Jimmy. Jimmy, I don't know why God won't take me. (JIMMY *kisses* THERESE MARIE *on her lips—it's a big-screen kiss.*) . . . Oh, Jimmy!

And JIMMY *vanishes.*

DANNY The doctors and nurses worked on my mother all night. And though my mother had only a barely discernible pulse, the medical team remained encouraged by the fact that despite the dire nature of her circumstances, she never stopped talking all night:

THERESE MARIE (*groggy*) Olivia de Havilland, Errol Flynn, 1938, a wonderful picture, Mr. Lincoln. Do you ever get to leave the White House, Mr. President? . . . I remember visiting my friend Norman in California—he took me to see the movie stars' homes. Do you remember that, Norman? (*Two men appear suddenly.*) (*snapping to*) Oh. Who are you?

BOBBY KENNEDY I'm Bobby Kennedy, and this is Pope John XXIII. We've come to collect my brother Jack's rightful vote from you for the 1960 election.

THERESE MARIE Oh, I'm so sorry, Bobby, but I didn't vote for your brother.

POPE JOHN XXIII *Mamma mia! Non credo!!*

THERESE MARIE But what did I do?

POPE JOHN XXIII According to Bobby here, you no vote Democratic since Franklin Roosevelt!

THERESE MARIE But I voted for McGovern.

BOBBY KENNEDY And gee—what a big help that was!

POPE JOHN XXIII You a nice Irish Catholic girl from Kearny, New Jersey—how you vote againsta fucka JFK?!

THERESE MARIE I don't know.

BOBBY KENNEDY Oh, cut the crap, narrowback. Of course you know—you vote Republican because your father was a lifelong Democrat! And you, you're so damaged that you'd rather mortgage your children's future by voting Republican than just confront your issues with your *slaphappy no-hear pappy!* C'mon! How bad could your pop have been? Ever hear of *Joe P. Kennedy,* lady? *My* father made Genghis Khan look like friggin' Chaka Khan, but that didn't stop me and my brothers from a lifetime of service to the lesser of the two evils—so what's your excuse?

THERESE MARIE (*shouts*) Oh, screw you, Bobby! Philandering blowhard twerp!

DANNY On October 14, 1899, in a tenement row house

somewhere between the Lincoln Tunnel and Grand Central Station, a deaf son was born to a pair of poor Irish immigrants newly arrived from County Cork. And although, by all accounts, my grandfather Francis James Sullivan possessed a brilliant mind, and read six newspapers a day till the day he died, he would be seen by those around him—as were all deaf people in those days—as a "dummy."

FRANCIS JAMES *appears. He is carrying a tremendous stack of newspapers, which he sets before* THERESE MARIE. *In his mouth, like a pacifier, is an old, stubby cigar. He dons a pair of spectacles and sits close by his daughter's side.*

He beckons her to recite from the day's headlines by pointing and tapping at a particular news item. This is a daily ritual between them—one they approach with real seriousness, but also with excitement and pleasure.

THERESE MARIE *is now four years old.*

THERESE MARIE "Lone Woman Flyer Lands in . . . Ear-Land."

FRANCIS JAMES *taps on the incorrect word forcefully, then pulls on his ear, shakes his head, and shrugs as if to say, "WHAT?!" He signs as he speaks:*

FRANCIS JAMES EAR-land?!
THERESE MARIE (*reconsidering*) "Lone Woman Flyer Lands in . . . Ear-UH-land."

FRANCIS JAMES *points to his eye emphatically.*

THERESE MARIE Eye? Eye what?

FRANCIS JAMES *shakes his head violently, makes the sign for "the Irish"—the fork in the potato.*

THERESE MARIE Fork in the potato? Fork. Oh. Irish. "Lone Woman Flyer Lands in IREland?"

FRANCIS JAMES *smiles.*

THERESE MARIE "Lone Woman Flyer Lands in IRELAND!"

FRANCIS JAMES *nods, points to the next headline with a* tap-tap-tap.

DANNY Being a "dummy" was bad enough. Being an Irish dummy was worse. But being a poor Irish dummy was to join ranks with the poor black dummies and the poor Italian and Jewish dummies forced to exist in a ghetto inside of a ghetto. The ghetto of poverty and silence and shadows. The ghetto of the broken back.

THERESE MARIE "Hunt for Murderer of Lindbergh Baby Turns to MARY-land." They're looking for Lindy's baby in Maryland!

FRANCIS JAMES *is very pleased.*

FRANCIS JAMES Who's the smartest four-year-old in Kearny, New Jersey!

THERESE MARIE I'm the smartest four-year-old in Kearny, New Jersey?—oh, I don't think so, Poppa.

FRANCIS JAMES *pats her head, beckons her to keep reading with a* tap-tap-tap *to the paper, and vanishes.*

DANNY And so on March 30, 1925, nine months after his marriage to the also deaf Sarah Martin of the teetotaling Martins of Providence, Rhode Island, Francis James pronounced before God and all of the assembled Sullivans the following edict—the first step in the fruition of a dream:

FRANCIS JAMES *speaks and signs.*

FRANCIS JAMES As God is my witness, my baby girl will become a teacher of the deaf!!

UNCLE BARNEY Teacher of the deaf! Franny's baby! Here, here!

FRANCIS JAMES And the conditions for the deaf will improve because of *my baby girl*!

UNCLE BARNEY Improved conditions, there can be no doubt!

FRANCIS JAMES And if someone has a problem with that, let them say it to *my face*!

AUNT MARGARET You tell 'em, Franny!

FRANCIS JAMES *I swear this on my life! Uh-oh.*

FRANCIS JAMES *collapses in a drunken stupor. A woman screams.* BARNEY *comes to his aid.*

AUNT MARGARET Oh, poor Francis! Give him some air!

UNCLE BARNEY Can the air, Marge—give 'im a whiskey!

And they all vanish.

DANNY My mother never became a teacher of the deaf.
Instead, she made a *promise*. And later she kept a *secret*.
And later still, she failed to do the work to repair the
damage of that secret—for *fear of being disloyal to the
dead* . . .

Blackout.

SCENE 2 • THREE DAYS LATER

THERESE MARIE *is praying a rosary. Next to the curtain-drawn
bed of her roommate,* MISS HALZIG, *her son,* DAVID HALZIG, *sits.
He is around forty-five to fifty, but looks both younger and
older than his age. He doesn't open the curtain to his mother's
bed; he just sits. He doesn't look around or read—he just sits.
His demeanor is near catatonic.*

ESPINOSA *enters with a newspaper.*

ESPINOSA (*to* THERESE MARIE) *Mami, qué pasa?*

THERESE MARIE Oh, hello. You're the boy with the smile.

ESPINOSA Espinosa. Yes. I brought you some mints, *mami.*

THERESE MARIE Thank you.

ESPINOSA And some Chessmen cookies too!

THERESE MARIE Oh—but I have no money to pay you.

ESPINOSA Everything in this life is not for money. I like you, so I buy. If I don't like you, *pppppppppppppffffff*! But I like you. No-name lady. Amnesia Mysteriosa!

THERESE MARIE Yes . . .

ESPINOSA (*to* DAVID HALZIG) Hey . . . Hey, *puto*! . . . *puto*! You read the *Post* already, *puto*?

DAVID HALZIG Huh?

ESPINOSA You want the *Post*?

DAVID HALZIG Oh. Yes. Thanks.

ESPINOSA You saw the game last night?

DAVID HALZIG Huh?

ESPINOSA The game, *pendejo*! Pedro! You saw it?

DAVID HALZIG Uh. No . . .

ESPINOSA Read about it: Pedro, mothahfuckah! Season of redemption! He's coming to get you!

DAVID HALZIG Pedro, huh?

ESPINOSA Das my word. Hey, you wanna donut, *puto*?

DAVID HALZIG No, thank you.

ESPINOSA They free, *puto*, it's not like I'm giving you nuthin'.

DAVID HALZIG Maybe later.

ESPINOSA Maybe later? Okay, *puto*. It ain't no thing . . . How's Mommy doing?

DAVID HALZIG Okay.

ESPINOSA Okay?!

DAVID HALZIG Yes.

ESPINOSA How you know that staring at a curtain? You got X-ray vision like a superhero?

DAVID HALZIG No.

ESPINOSA You *Superputo*?

DAVID HALZIG No, I . . .

ESPINOSA *Cálmate, puto* . . . Here. (*Hands him a donut.*) Here. Break it up in little pieces. She'll eat it. She likes cinnamon. When you're ready. Okay?

DAVID HALZIG Thanks.

ESPINOSA Whatever.

DAVID HALZIG That's very nice of you.

ESPINOSA Whatever . . . Okay, *puto*: read about Pedro.

DAVID HALZIG Yes . . . Uh, who's "Pedro"?

ESPINOSA "Who's Pedro"?!

DAVID HALZIG Who is he?

ESPINOSA Whatsamatter, you got something wrong with your mind?

DAVID HALZIG No.

ESPINOSA Everybody know about Pedro. Even the old lady, she know about Pedro. In *China*, muthahfuckah—you know China?

DAVID HALZIG Yeah.

ESPINOSA In *China*, they know about Pedro. So, what happen to your mind you don't know Pedro?

DAVID HALZIG Uh, I don't watch much television.

ESPINOSA Then read about it, *puto*. Let's go, Mets! Okay, *puto*?

DAVID HALZIG Okay.

ESPINOSA Okay, *puto*. Very good. (*Starts to exit.*)

DAVID HALZIG Hey?

ESPINOSA What?

DAVID HALZIG What's *puto*?

ESPINOSA *Puto*? You know—it means, like, "friend."

DAVID HALZIG Oh.

ESPINOSA You got Latino doormen in your building?

DAVID HALZIG Yes.

ESPINOSA When they open the door for you, tell 'em: "Thanks, *puto.*"

DAVID HALZIG Okay. I'll do that.

ESPINOSA Okay. I'll check you later, *puto.* Read about Pedro.

ESPINOSA *goes to exit.*

DR. SHANKAR *enters with* DETECTIVE BAKER *in street clothes.*

DR. SHANKAR Espinosa, the second-floor restroom is overflowing like a sewer.

ESPINOSA (*half audible as he exits*) Call Roto-Rooter, mothahfuckah.

DR. SHANKAR (*to* DETECTIVE BAKER) Right this way. (*to* THERESE MARIE) Good morning.

THERESE MARIE Oh. Good morning.

DR. SHANKAR How you feeling this morning?

THERESE MARIE Not great. Can you tell me your name?

DR. SHANKAR I told you my name yesterday and the day before and the day before—I'm Dr. Shankar.

THERESE MARIE Can you speak a little louder?

DR. SHANKAR I'm Dr. Shankar.

THERESE MARIE Stanker?

DR. SHANKAR Shankar. Like lamb "shank" plus a "car."

THERESE MARIE Could you spell it, please?

DR. SHANKAR S-H-A-N—

THERESE MARIE M?

DR. SHANKAR N . . . S-H-A-N-K-A-R.

THERESE MARIE Oh. Shankar. Like beef shanks—

DR. SHANKAR "Shank"—plus a "car." Yes . . . And what is your name, dear?

THERESE MARIE They keep asking me, Dr. Shag-Heart, but I don't know.

DR. SHANKAR Have you ever been to the nursing home at the Department of Aging? It's not a nice place, but that's where we have to send people who don't know—or won't disclose—their identities.

THERESE MARIE "Won't disclose"?

DR. SHANKAR This is a man who's gonna see if he can help you jog your memory. We're all hoping he's successful— we don't like to send people to the Department of Aging.

THERESE MARIE I don't want to be any trouble, Doctor.

DR. SHANKAR And yet, you are . . . (*Exits.*)

DETECTIVE BAKER Smug little fella, ain't he?

THERESE MARIE A bit of a cold fish, yes.

DETECTIVE BAKER I'm going to take a photo of you now. Is that okay?

THERESE MARIE Oh, I hate to have my picture taken.

DETECTIVE BAKER You shouldn't—you're a very pretty lady.

THERESE MARIE I'm a fat old bag.

He snaps a photo.

DETECTIVE BAKER There we are . . . Say, are those cookies in your plastic bag there?

THERESE MARIE Oh. Yes.

DETECTIVE BAKER May I?

THERESE MARIE Oh, please. Can you tell me your name?

DETECTIVE BAKER Baker. B-A-K-E-R.

THERESE MARIE Baker.

DETECTIVE BAKER Yes.

THERESE MARIE There was a song about a baker once.

(*singing*)
You baked me
You creped me
You triple-layer-caked me
You're the baker of my heart.

DETECTIVE BAKER You have a great memory for a gal your age.

THERESE MARIE It comes and goes.

DETECTIVE BAKER Say, I heard they found a book of crossword puzzles in your bag when they brought you in.

THERESE MARIE Did they? I don't know.

DETECTIVE BAKER Do you do crosswords?

THERESE MARIE Sometimes, I guess. To pass the time.

DETECTIVE BAKER This book of crosswords was all filled in—a very smart lady with a very good memory must have done those crosswords.

THERESE MARIE Sometimes they're easy.

DETECTIVE BAKER This was a Sunday *New York Times* crossword puzzle book. I don't know if anyone would say that those are easy.

THERESE MARIE I really can't say.

DETECTIVE BAKER I need to ask you what you were doing up at the Cloisters last week.

THERESE MARIE Was I at the Cloisters??

DETECTIVE BAKER Were you attacked? Mugged? Assaulted in some manner?

THERESE MARIE No.

DETECTIVE BAKER You sure about that?

THERESE MARIE Yes.

DETECTIVE BAKER You're telling me you're sure you weren't attacked, but yet you can't remember your own name?

THERESE MARIE . . . I wish I could help you, Mr. Baker.

DETECTIVE BAKER It's funny. You can remember *my* name. You can remember no one mugged you. You can even remember a song from yesteryears gone by. It's very puzzling. You some kind of fugitive from justice? Is that it? Ma Barker's second cousin Machine Gun Mildred, sumpthin' like that?

THERESE MARIE It would certainly be exciting if I was.

DETECTIVE BAKER Hmmm . . . And may I assume that your wedding ring there isn't inscribed?

THERESE MARIE Would you like to see it?

DETECTIVE BAKER No. That'd be too easy, wouldn't it?

THERESE MARIE I'm happy to show it to you.

DETECTIVE BAKER Of course you are—'cuz it don't say jack, does it?

THERESE MARIE I'm afraid not.

Beat.

DETECTIVE BAKER Show me the ring.

THERESE MARIE Here.

DETECTIVE BAKER Okay . . . Well, I'll tell you one thing: If I had a secret, you'd be the one I'd tell. Is your husband deceased?

THERESE MARIE He is.

DETECTIVE BAKER My wife passed ten years ago.

THERESE MARIE I'm sorry.

DETECTIVE BAKER How'd you meet your husband?

THERESE MARIE . . . I worked for the airlines. TWA. I was so fortunate. I got to see the world. We met overseas. A confirmed bachelor and an old maid. He looked just like Lorne Greene.

DETECTIVE BAKER So what's your name, lady?

FRANCIS JAMES *appears. He watches.*

THERESE MARIE Ooo. Ooo. I'm sorry, but I'm in an awful lot of pain.

DETECTIVE BAKER I'm sorry about that.

THERESE MARIE Can you get the nurse, please? I've been ringing, but no one has come.

DETECTIVE BAKER Come for what?

THERESE MARIE I'm sorry, but I need to make a bowel movement.

DETECTIVE BAKER Okay . . . Well, can I bring you something when I come back?

THERESE MARIE No, thank you.

DETECTIVE BAKER Nothing at all?

THERESE MARIE I'd love a scotch. Johnnie Walker.

DETECTIVE BAKER Well, maybe once we're on a first-name basis.

ESPINOSA *enters.*

ESPINOSA Somebody rang?

THERESE MARIE I'm awfully sorry, I feel I need to make a bowel movement.

ESPINOSA And I feel I need to help someone to make a bowel movement—whaddya think of that, *mi amor*?

THERESE MARIE I'm sorry, but is there a nurse?

ESPINOSA It's okay, *mami*, I do bowel movements—it's, like, a specialty of mines.

THERESE MARIE I'm embarrassed.

ESPINOSA Well, I could go get Esther to come in and help you, but Esther, she kinda rough—you met her?

THERESE MARIE I'm not sure.

ESPINOSA If you did, you'd remember. She's a brute. She don't got the touch like me. Believe me, *mami*, I got a Ph.D. in ass. You gotta lotta pain, right?

THERESE MARIE Yes.

ESPINOSA Then you better stick with the Ph.D. Okay?

THERESE MARIE Okay.

DETECTIVE BAKER I'll be back later, ma'am.

ESPINOSA (*to* DETECTIVE BAKER) Yo, Officer, you comin' back later?

DETECTIVE BAKER It's "Detective"—and yeah, I'll be back later. Why?

ESPINOSA You could bring me back a slice and a pack a Newports?

DETECTIVE BAKER Uh . . . Sure, I guess.

ESPINOSA And some Ho Hos. Not Yodels—Ho Hos.

DETECTIVE BAKER Got it.

ESPINOSA And a Fanta, and here, get something for yourself.

DETECTIVE BAKER That's okay.

ESPINOSA A coffee, something—whatever. Beef patty.

DETECTIVE BAKER Okay then.

ESPINOSA Anyways, no rush, Officer, do your duties, whatever. "Protect and Serve." I'm with dat.

THERESE MARIE Mr. Baker—you're with the police?

DETECTIVE BAKER As if you didn't know.

THERESE MARIE Am I in some sort of trouble?

DETECTIVE BAKER I sure hope so. I wouldn't mind one last big collar 'fore I fade into the sunset . . . All right then, I'll be back. (*Exits.*)

ESPINOSA Okay, *mi amor*, now I'm gonna take this pot, put it under your ass, okay?

THERESE MARIE Okay.

ESPINOSA *very methodically completes the procedure.*

ESPINOSA Did you feel that?

THERESE MARIE No.

ESPINOSA No pain or discomfort getting the pot under there?

THERESE MARIE No.

ESPINOSA Ph.D. . . .

THERESE MARIE Yes. Thanks.

ESPINOSA Okay then. I'll be back. (*to* DAVID HALZIG) Yo, *puto*?

DAVID HALZIG Huh?

ESPINOSA Do you enjoy watchin' people try to make their business?

DAVID HALZIG No.

ESPINOSA Well then, come on, les go, *puto*—take a walk, *cabrón*, circulate your ass.

DAVID HALZIG Circulate. Yes.

ESPINOSA (*to* THERESE MARIE, on the exit) Perimeter secured, *mami.* Don't be shy.

Lights fade.

SCENE 3

A motel somewhere outside Cleveland. Night. NADINE, *using a lighter and empty Bic pen, is smoking black-tar heroin resin off a piece of aluminum foil. She is sitting on the floor. Next to her is a Slurpee and a little iPod boombox. The song "Bron-Yr-Aur" by Led Zeppelin cuts the silence.*

DANNY *is lying on the bed, fully dressed and at a loss.*

DANNY . . . I should've killed that motherfucker!

NADINE It's hitchhiking, Danny. It goes with the territory.

DANNY That fuckin' animal—I swear to God, I don't know how he escaped with his fuckin' life!

NADINE It's 'cuz you're a good person, Danny.

DANNY I'm not a good person.

NADINE You're a really good person, and you should really consider smoking some of this.

DANNY I don't wanna.

NADINE I'm just saying, like: "Just say no"—there's obviously a lot of validity to it, but in certain circumstances, like how you're feeling right now with your mom and all, I'd make a strong,

nonenabling argument for "Just say yes" . . .
Ya know?

Beat.

DANNY . . . I just don't want her to be dead!

NADINE I know.

DANNY I should've never left her!

NADINE . . . C'mere.

DANNY No.

NADINE Can I play you a song?

DANNY My mother could be dead, Nadine. She could be
anywhere. Okay?!

NADINE *turns off the music.*

NADINE Danny, you almost just killed a guy who was willing
to take us all the way to Jersey because he asked me if he
could watch me lick my tits. I woulda licked my tits to get
us to Jersey, and you almost killed him!

DANNY What's your point?

NADINE My point is: Come here and sit down.

DANNY *complies.*

NADINE Have a sip of this.

DANNY What is it?

NADINE It's a Slurpee . . . with gin.

He drinks.

DANNY It's good.

She shuffles to find a song.

NADINE I really wish we coulda seen Elvis's house.

DANNY We're not on a field trip, Nadine.

NADINE Not for me, Danny. For you.

DANNY Why? You been there?

NADINE Well, I didn't actually go inside the house.

DANNY No?

NADINE It was closed. But . . . outside the house, there's this big wall that surrounds it, and everybody, like all the tourists, they're allowed to write graffiti on the wall, like, notes to Elvis and stuff.

DANNY Uh-huh.

NADINE Yeah. So I start reading the wall, and it was amazing, but thousands of pieces of graffiti, maybe more than thousands, and not one person wrote, like, "Hey fatso, you died of a heart attack while you were tryin' ta take a shit" . . . I mean you figure there's gotta be at least one clown at the circus, ya know? But there was nothing negative at all. Nothing. And I don't know why, but I found the whole thing . . . comforting . . . Ya know?

DANNY Um.

NADINE *hits Play. It's "Little Greenie" by Gary Jules.*

NADINE Okay . . . One time, I was gonna kill myself, but then I played this Gary Jules song like twenty-seven times.

The song plays. During that time, they have a moment, then start smoking the tar. One person holding the foil and lighting it, the other with the pen, and back and forth as the lights fade.

SCENE 4 • HOSPITAL. LATER THAT NIGHT.

MAGNOLIA *is changing the sheets, and adjusting* THERESE MARIE*'s position as she does so.* DETECTIVE BAKER *sits in the chair with two coffee cups of wine.*

THERESE MARIE Owww! It hurts, it hurts!

MAGNOLIA Listen, dear: if this is a pity party you throwin', I will not be attending!

THERESE MARIE Oh, it hurts.

MAGNOLIA I'm sorry for that. Don't fight me and it will be over faster, right, dear?

THERESE MARIE I'm sorry. I'm sorry.

MAGNOLIA That's okay. Now we gonna turn.

THERESE MARIE Aaaaaaaaaaaah!!

MAGNOLIA That's an opera you singing?

THERESE MARIE Pain! Pain! Ooww! Please! Don't move me!

MAGNOLIA Listen now: "We are pressed on every side by troubles, but we are not crushed and broken." (*Flips* THERESE MARIE *deftly on her side.*)

THERESE MARIE Oh my God. Oh my God.

MAGNOLIA Second Corinthians, chapter 4, verse 8. Breathe now. You breathing?

THERESE MARIE You're a tough SOB, aren't you?

MAGNOLIA Tough 'cuz I have to be. (*to* DETECTIVE BAKER) She should *not* be drinking.

THERESE MARIE Oh, live a little.

MAGNOLIA That's what I'm trying to do: make sure everybody live.

DR. SHANKAR *enters in a tuxedo.*

MAGNOLIA Oh. Good evening, Doctor.

DR. SHANKAR Good evening.

MAGNOLIA You look very handsome, Doctor.

DR. SHANKAR Yes. I came from a benefit.

THERESE MARIE Who's that?

DR. SHANKAR Leave me alone with her, would you?

MAGNOLIA Yes, Doctor.

DR. SHANKAR *hands* MAGNOLIA *a platter covered in aluminum foil.*

DR. SHANKAR Shrimp, stuffed mushrooms, and some rubber chicken breasts. You can leave it out in the nurse's station if anyone wants.

MAGNOLIA How kind.

DR. SHANKAR Yes. Thank you, Mongolia.

MAGNOLIA *exits.* DR. SHANKAR *approaches* THERESE MARIE.

DR. SHANKAR And how are you this fair evening?

THERESE MARIE *doesn't recognize him in the tuxedo.*

THERESE MARIE Who are you?

DR. SHANKAR I'm your doctor. Who are you?

THERESE MARIE I'm afraid we haven't had much luck figuring that out.

DR. SHANKAR Good evening, Detective.

DETECTIVE BAKER Evening, Doc. We were just talkin' about Joe Louis. Isn't that right?

THERESE MARIE He restored our nation's honor.

DETECTIVE BAKER Got that right. (*to* DR. SHANKAR) Ever heard about the Brown Bomber, Doc?

DR. SHANKAR May I sit down?

THERESE MARIE Oh, please do—would you like a mint?

DR. SHANKAR No, thank you.

THERESE MARIE I'm sorry, Doctor, but do you have a brother?

DR. SHANKAR A brother? No.

THERESE MARIE Because there's a doctor here that looks just like you—you have the same jaw, the same eyes—

DR. SHANKAR Is he a good doctor, this doctor?

THERESE MARIE Oh, he's a jackass, if you really want to know. I've been treated by hundreds of doctors, Doctor—I spent ten years in charity hospitals from Newark to East Orange—

DR. SHANKAR Yes, well . . . I'm sorry you don't like me.

THERESE MARIE . . . Like "you"?

DR. SHANKAR You don't know who I am?

THERESE MARIE . . . Oh, my! . . . Oh Jesus, Mary, and Joseph, Dr. Shag-Heart—I'm so sorry.

DR. SHANKAR (*re:* THERESE MARIE) I see someone's been drinking a little wine.

DETECTIVE BAKER (*covering*) Why yes—I noticed that too.

DR. SHANKAR You wanna make it all up to me, dear? Tell me who you are.

DETECTIVE BAKER Good luck, Doc.

DR. SHANKAR Your children have a right to know where their mother is.

THERESE MARIE I don't have children.

DR. SHANKAR You have scars from two Cesarean sections. Are your children deceased? Is that what you're telling me?

THERESE MARIE Oh, I'll be gone soon anyway.

DR. SHANKAR Perhaps. However—

THERESE MARIE I'm really in a lot of pain, and I want to rest now.

DR. SHANKAR Detective Baker tells me you like scotch.

THERESE MARIE Yes, but . . .

Dr. Shankar produces a small bottle and some glasses.

DR. SHANKAR I'm going to take off my tie, okay?

THERESE MARIE Okay.

DR. SHANKAR Pour us a coupla very tiny scotches and have a talk.

THERESE MARIE About what?

DR. SHANKAR *pours her a scotch. She sips.*

THERESE MARIE Ah—heaven.

DR. SHANKAR Yes. Scotch is nice.

THERESE MARIE Sheer heaven!

DR. SHANKAR Now. Do you remember the CAT scan we took two days ago? And then the MRI?

THERESE MARIE You found something.

DR. SHANKAR Your children should be notified.

THERESE MARIE Am I dying?

DR. SHANKAR *sips, then:*

DR. SHANKAR Everybody's dying, miss. Look at me:
Vigorous. Vital. Physically fit. Dying. That's what's called
the human condition.

THERESE MARIE Yes, I know about the human condition, but
what about me?

DR. SHANKAR You should think about your children.

THERESE MARIE When will I go, Doctor? Soon?

DR. SHANKAR *looks to* DETECTIVE BAKER. DETECTIVE BAKER
considers.

Beat.

DETECTIVE BAKER I believe that's not in the doctor's power to
say. Isn't that right, Doc?

DR. SHANKAR Yes. It's not.

DETECTIVE BAKER And yet, sounds like "a word to the wise is
sufficient," as they say.

Beat.

THERESE MARIE I'll need a priest.

DR. SHANKAR *rises.*

DR. SHANKAR And who shall I say is asking for him?

THERESE MARIE I just . . . It's an unbearable thing to be a burden on your children, Doctor.

DR. SHANKAR I understand.

THERESE MARIE Terrible and unbearable.

DR. SHANKAR Yes.

Beat.

THERESE MARIE My name is Therese Sullivan O'Connor. Terry. I live with my son, Danny, at 440 Riverside Drive. But my daughter Justina has been taking care of me while he's been away.

DR. SHANKAR Good. Very good . . . Now look at me, Terry.

THERESE MARIE Yes?

DR. SHANKAR I have some very good news.

THERESE MARIE Yes?

DR. SHANKAR Despite whatever you think you might have just heard, which, I should point out, I never did say, you are not dying. At least not yet. Although you could die. But I don't think so.

THERESE MARIE What?

DETECTIVE BAKER I'm gonna go run that name right now. Very nice meeting ya, Terry. (*to* DR. SHANKAR) And you, Cool Hand Luke, that was some stone-cold you-know-what. I'm impressed . . . All right now. (*Exits.*)

THERESE MARIE So . . . So . . . I'm not . . .

DR. SHANKAR No. Nothing to fear. (*Exits.*)

THERESE MARIE . . . Oh hell. (*Begins to weep, as lights fade.*) Oh hell . . .

SCENE 5 • THE NEXT EVENING

MAGNOLIA *enters with a tray of food.* DANNY *and* NADINE *are seated at the bedside.* THERESE MARIE *is asleep.*

MAGNOLIA Time for eating now, Therese. (*Goes to rouse* THERESE MARIE.)

NADINE Um, she's sleeping.

MAGNOLIA Sleeping when she should be eating, yes.

DANNY Could you leave it? I'll make sure she eats.

MAGNOLIA *considers this, then acquiesces.*

MAGNOLIA She's a tough lady.

DANNY Yup.

MAGNOLIA No. I mean tough to deal with. She tell me today she was named after Saint Thérèse, the Little Flower. You know, the nice one? I told her they shoulda named her after that ruffian Teresa of Ávila instead! (*Laughs heartily.*) You sonny boy?

DANNY Yeah.

MAGNOLIA She have God in her clear as day, sonny boy. Make sure she eat.

MAGNOLIA *exits.*

THERESE MARIE *stirs, wakes.*

Beat.

THERESE MARIE . . . Danny?

DANNY Hey, Mom.

THERESE MARIE . . . Oh, Danny—Danny—I didn't want you to come!

DANNY Well, here I am.

THERESE MARIE Did you speak to the doctor?

DANNY Ma—I just got here.

THERESE MARIE Don't you want to take off your coat?

DANNY Mom—

THERESE MARIE You look terrible, Danny.

DANNY How am I supposed to look?

THERESE MARIE Don't snap.

DANNY I'm not snapping.

THERESE MARIE Danny, you weren't supposed to come.

DANNY Justina's downstairs.

THERESE MARIE Did she speak to the doctor? Is she coming up?

DANNY She's in the lobby. She's really fuckin' pissed, Mom.

THERESE MARIE Oh, Danny—don't curse like that.

DANNY Mom—

THERESE MARIE When you use that foul language, it's like you're sneezing on my arm!

DANNY Sorry—

THERESE MARIE —Now where's Justina?

DANNY I just told you—

THERESE MARIE —Well, where is she?!

DANNY Downstairs!

THERESE MARIE Well, is she coming up?

DANNY I don't know if she's coming up, Mom, she's really, really fucking upset!

THERESE MARIE Poor thing. Of course she's upset. I feel awful! Just awful! She's always hated me, Danny. Even when she loved me, it was in spite of herself!

DANNY Yeah, well, running away from home like a fuckin' maniac doesn't do much to iron out those outstanding mother-daughter issues, Mom.

THERESE MARIE . . . I was thinking about her violin lessons the other day: do you remember the horror we endured?!

DANNY I'm gonna go have a cigarette.

THERESE MARIE I love you, Danny. Come take my hand.

DANNY You're out of your fuckin' mind, Mom.

NADINE Don't say that, Danny.

THERESE MARIE (*re:* NADINE) Danny, who's this? A new friend?

DANNY It doesn't matter who she is! What does "who she is" have to do with anything at all right now?!

THERESE MARIE Danny—you're yelling.

DANNY I'm yelling 'cuz you're making me yell! I'm yelling because my mother fell off the face of the earth for a fuckin' week—Mom—and then when we finally find her—which is goddamn well what she wanted us to do in the first place—when we finally find her—after losing our minds and after our lives have been tossed to the fuckin' lions—when I finally fuckin' see her—all she can say is "Oh, Danny, I didn't want you to come" and "Who's your new fuckin' friend"!

THERESE MARIE I'm sorry, Danny, but I'm in an awful lot of pain, and I think you need to go home and get some sleep now.

DANNY I need to get some sleep?!

THERESE MARIE Go home, Danny.

DANNY I just traveled two thousand miles not knowing if you were dead or alive, Mom, and now, just because I can't instantly flip into "do whatever Mom wants" mode and take your hand and take off my coat and answer your questions, I'm supposed to just turn around and go the fuck home because you say so?!

THERESE MARIE I almost died in here, Danny—I had to be *revived*—and you're popping off at me like some kind of nasty barroom hothead!!

DANNY And why the fuck do you think that is, Mom?!

THERESE MARIE Danny, the language—

DANNY Fuck you "the language"!! You're out of your fuckin' mind, you're completely out of adjustment with reality, and it's not *fair*, okay?! *What the fuck is the matter with you?! Goddamnit!*

DANNY *storms out.*

Pause.

NADINE . . . Um . . . I don't know what they're giving you, but I've got some really good drugs if you're in pain.

THERESE MARIE (*re:* DANNY) He's just overtired, is all.

NADINE I know.

THERESE MARIE He feels things too deeply.

NADINE I know . . . um, I know you're in the hospital and you're in a lot of pain, and you might be dying and all, but you're really very pretty, Miss O'Connor. You don't look your age at all.

FRANCIS JAMES *appears. He is withdrawn, preoccupied.*

NADINE (*re:* FRANCIS JAMES) Uh, Miss O'Connor—who's that?

THERESE MARIE You can see him?

NADINE Yeah—I been smoking black-tar heroin pretty much around the clock since we left Scottsdale, so I'm kind of attuned to lots of things and energies and stuff that aren't really there in the actual world of people who aren't fucked up, dying, or just plain whacked.

THERESE MARIE I see . . . What did you say your name was, honey?

NADINE Nadine.

THERESE MARIE Nay-deen?

NADINE Yeah. Nadine Powers.

THERESE MARIE Powers? Like the whiskey?

NADINE Prolly. Yeah.

Pause.

THERESE MARIE . . . Don't get old, Nadine.

NADINE Yeah, uh—I don't think I'm headed in that direction, but I'll definitely keep it in mind . . .
(*re:* FRANCIS JAMES) *So, who's that guy over there?*

THERESE MARIE He's my father.

NADINE Oh.

THERESE MARIE Danny's grandfather.

NADINE Oh . . . Do you think he'd wanna smoke some pot?

THERESE MARIE I don't think so, no.

NADINE Um . . . Do you think he'd mind if *I* smoked some pot?

THERESE MARIE Um, honey, I don't think it's a good idea to smoke pot here in the hospital.

NADINE Oh . . . okay . . . Your father looks very stern.

THERESE MARIE Not "stern," honey—perplexed. The poor man is terribly perplexed.

DANNY *speaks to the audience.*

DANNY I went downstairs to get my sister, Justina, but she was gone. I called her up and met her at a bar down the block.

Note: They play the dialogue from opposite ends of the stage, not in a "real" bar.

JUSTINA This bar is disgusting, Danny. The smell is hurting my sinuses.

DANNY I met *you* here.

JUSTINA Did you speak to the doctor?

DANNY No. I went to find you.

JUSTINA You didn't speak to the doctor?!

DANNY I was going to—

JUSTINA Well, I mean, is she okay?

DANNY You should go see her.

JUSTINA Why? Is she dying? Is she dying, Danny—you better fuckin' tell me!!

DANNY I didn't speak to the doctor, but—

JUSTINA Oh my God! What did she do? What the fuck is wrong with her?! Why is my whole family a fuckin' disaster?!

DANNY Listen to me: I don't think she's dying.

JUSTINA Then fuck her! I'm sorry, but fuck her! I gotta call work. And who the fuck is that little blonde?!

She vanishes.

DANNY *speaks.*

DANNY I stayed in the bar after my sister left. Seven and sevens. Dollar drafts. Some guy with bad coke. I couldn't deal with going right back to the hospital. After a while, Nadine met me. We bought a tray of drinks and sat in a back booth where it was dark and did a good job at forgetting . . . I don't remember who it was who said, "I never saw a wild thing sorry for itself," but Nadine had that quality in spades. Her lithium and clozapine prescriptions were running out, as was the dope, but we walked arm in arm in the light of grace despite it. It was late, but the night guy at the hospital let us back in. We told him we had just got off a plane. He said I was a good son.

Faint lights come up on THERESE MARIE*'s room. Darkness. Passage of time.* THERESE MARIE *is out cold.*

JUSTINA *enters. She is unpacking a violin.*

DANNY . . . My sister Justina, she was born seven years later than me, and seven years is a long space of time when your parents were old when they started having kids in the first place.

JUSTINA *tunes her violin.*

DANNY My mom had me at forty. But she was forty-seven by the time she had Justina. And somehow my sister was born believing that her parents' days were numbered. She used to wake up from nightmares in the middle of the night and sneak into their bedroom—not for comfort, but to make sure they were still breathing. This is true. And what started out as a source of terror for her slowly began evolving into a source of anger—much of that anger being directed at my mom.

She bursts into tears and begins playing an Irish fox-trot.

JUSTINA (*to her unconscious mom*) I fuckin' hate you! (*Plays.*) Fuckin' "Face of Poverty" dumb Irish bitch! (*And plays.*) Fuckin' pathetic, helpless martyr! (*And plays.*) If you die, I won't bury you!

She plays. And cries. And plays. And cries.

DANNY *enters with* NADINE. *He just watches. After a moment, he sits by his mom's side.*

JUSTINA I hate you too, Danny.

DANNY I know.

JUSTINA No, I'm serious—I fuckin' hate you.

DANNY Okay.

JUSTINA Get clean, for Chrissakes—and lose the jailbait.

DANNY Okay.

JUSTINA Look at her sleeping—oblivious bitch.

DANNY As we sat here on this night—my mom sleeping, my sister playing the violin, Nadine nodding out, everybody being nice—grace had entered the room. And even during all the decisions and talks and thoughts and fights that led to my being where I am, and Mom being where she is, and Justina being left all alone—grace never left. And what is "grace"? . . . Grace, to me, is that thing that I constantly spit in the face of. If there's a God, he loves me. But I don't seem to love him back enough. And thus: my life . . . Grace offered acceptance and good counsel. And I spit in the face of it. Why? 'Cuz somehow I felt . . . I don't know . . . undeserving . . . and angry, and completely fuckin' powerless.

FRANCIS JAMES *appears.*

DANNY Like a deaf, drunk, God-fearing, child-beating, willful shanty Irishman during the Depression.

THERESE MARIE *calls out in her sleep.*

THERESE MARIE . . . Danny?

JUSTINA *keeps playing as the lights fade.*

ACT 2

SCENE 1 • THE HOSPITAL. MIDSTREAM.

DANNY . . . Anyways, Mom, I'm sorry about yesterday.

THERESE MARIE Where's the little girl?

DANNY I put her on the Circle Line. She likes boats. (*Beat.*)
  What happened to your, uh, roommate?

THERESE MARIE I don't know. They took her out, I guess.

DANNY Oh . . .

THERESE MARIE Honey?

DANNY Yeah?

THERESE MARIE I want to see you.

DANNY I'm right here, Ma.

THERESE MARIE Come closer.

DANNY I'm pretty close right now, Mom.

THERESE MARIE Danny, stop it—I want to see your face.

DANNY You can't see my face?

THERESE MARIE I want to hold your hand and see
  your face.

DANNY . . . Okay . . . How's this?

THERESE MARIE There you are . . . Hello, honey boy.

DANNY Hi, Mom.

THERESE MARIE You're such a handsome boy, Danny.

DANNY Yes. Very handsome. A rake.

THERESE MARIE Yes you are! You're my beautiful, handsome boy. A handsome man!

DANNY Yes.

THERESE MARIE Hands just like your father, God rest his soul.

DANNY Uh-huh.

THERESE MARIE I love you so much, Danny—in a million years you could never know how much.

DANNY I love you too, Mom.

THERESE MARIE You, your father, and Justina—I'm the luckiest woman in the world!

DANNY We just want you to be okay, Mom.

THERESE MARIE Oh, honey, I'm fine. It's you I worry about.

DANNY Well, I'm fine too.

THERESE MARIE You're under a lot of stress and strain— horrible stress—terrible strain—I know.

DANNY I'm okay, Mom. Really.

Beat.

THERESE MARIE Honey . . . Can I *ask* you something, honey?

DANNY . . . Um, honestly, you *could* ask me something if, like, you really feel you *have* to, but if you could maybe, like, refrain from asking me something for just, like, a little bit, it might work out best that way for the both of us, ya know?

THERESE MARIE Danny, I just want to ask—because I think it's important—and you can tell me to just butt out if you want, but can I just ask: How is *Lucy*, have you spoken with her at all?

DANNY What?

THERESE MARIE I mean, honey, you can just tell me I'm a Nosy Susan if you want to.

DANNY You're a Nosy Susan, Mom.

THERESE MARIE So you haven't seen her?

DANNY . . . No, Ma. Okay?

THERESE MARIE Have you spoken to her?

DANNY No, not really.

THERESE MARIE What does that mean?

DANNY It just means I haven't really talked to her.

THERESE MARIE Oh. Okay . . . I just thought you might have spoken to her or seen her, you know, while you were away on your trip.

DANNY I wasn't on a "trip," Mom, I was in rehab.

THERESE MARIE Oh, honey, I know you were in rehab, I just thought, you know, you might have seen her or spoken to her.

DANNY No, Ma. Lucy lives in L.A., I was in Scottsdale, which, Scottsdale's not L.A. Scottsdale's Scottsdale . . .

THERESE MARIE Oh, I know, honey. But . . . how is she? Do you know?

DANNY Um, she's really good, I hear, okay?

THERESE MARIE Oh, I hope so, she was such a lovely girl.

DANNY Very lovely, yeah.

THERESE MARIE A family girl.

DANNY Family, yes.

THERESE MARIE Drop-dead gorgeous, I remember that—oh, those curves, remember? That smile!—but still, she was a real family girl. Genuine.

DANNY You hungry? I could go get ya something.

THERESE MARIE I still pray for her, you know.

DANNY I know you do, Ma, that's very bipartisan of you.

THERESE MARIE Oh, honey, it's not about being "bipartisan." It's nothing like that! I just ask God every day that whatever would be the best outcome for the both of you—for the *both* of you as *individuals*—I ask God to let whatever would be *best* for *each* of you be the thing that happens whether you get back together or not.

DANNY Well, God's definitely hearing 50 percent of your prayers, Ma, 'cuz she's doing, like, perfect . . .

THERESE MARIE Oh, I hope so. She was so lovely.

DANNY Yup.

THERESE MARIE Just lovely.

DANNY Uh-huh.

THERESE MARIE She was just crazy for you, Danny.

DANNY Yup. Can we, like, segue at this point, Mom?

THERESE MARIE . . . You know, Tala told me that she saw her in that movie—oh—what movie was that, Danny?

DANNY I really got no idea, Ma.

THERESE MARIE Anyway, I think Tala said she saw her in that movie, and you know, Tala said Lucy had a really rather good-sized part and that she was really very good.

DANNY That's great.

THERESE MARIE What movie was that, Danny?

DANNY Mom, I didn't go to the movies with Tala, so I don't know, and really—

THERESE MARIE —Something—oh, what was it—something about ghost lizards or reptile apparitions?

DANNY I don't know.

THERESE MARIE Or with fangs—bloody fangs—but from outer space or phantoms and ugly, ugly—

DANNY —Mom . . .

THERESE MARIE I just hope it led to something for her—it's very hard for women in show business, Danny.

DANNY I know, Ma.

THERESE MARIE I'm not saying it's not hard for men, but for women—too many vultures, users, two-bit snake oil salesmen: they take what they want from the women, then treat them like day-old baloney—just discarded—oh, it's just terrible, terrible. I worry about her.

DANNY She's doing really well, Mom. Okay? Trust me when I tell you: she's doing very, very, very well.

THERESE MARIE You still care for her deeply, Danny, don't you?

DANNY Actually, no, Ma, I don't—and it's been, like, three fuckin' years, so—

THERESE MARIE —Oh, three years, three minutes! I saw the way she used to look at you, Danny—and the way you looked at her—a woman knows that look

DANNY Okay, well, do you know *this* look, Ma?

THERESE MARIE Oh, honey. I'm sorry—

DANNY —It's okay, okay?! Let's just, uh, move on to some other painful, debilitating subject now if that's okay.

THERESE MARIE . . . I guess I just always hoped that the two of you might come to some reconciliation—

DANNY Mom, honestly, this'd be the optimal moment to fuckin' drop it, okay?

THERESE MARIE I just want you to be happy, Danny.

DANNY I'm very happy, Ma.

THERESE MARIE No you're not. You're miserable and upset and deeply, deeply depressed.

DANNY And if that's true, Mom—it has nothing to do with Lucy, okay?

THERESE MARIE Honey, love has no expiration date.

DANNY What?!

THERESE MARIE I just thought maybe while you were away maybe you'd see her and the two of you might find—

DANNY There's nothing to find, Ma, okay?! There's nothing! She lives in L.A. and I live here! And the fuckin' truth, Ma, is that the minute we weren't together anymore was the exact minute that her whole fuckin' life improved *dramatically*, Mom—not, "oh, it improved *slightly*"—I'm talkin' huge, gigantic "dreams come true," "all the sounds of the earth are like music," "a little brown maverick is winking its fuckin' eye" *quantum leap improvement* on every fuckin' level—okay?

THERESE MARIE Danny, people are trying to sleep.

DANNY If people are tryin' ta sleep, Mom, and you *know* that they're trying ta sleep, then why do you persist in a line of fuckin' questioning that's gonna elicit this kind of reaction from me?! Huh?! You *know* I don't like talking about Lucy with you—even when things were good I didn't like talking about her with you—and yet, despite the fact that there's like ten thousand other issues far more pertinent to present-day reality, and despite the fact that I am doing my level fuckin' best not to call you on shit that I *know* will only upset you, *you*, on the other hand, just think it's okay to talk about whatever you wanna talk about and ask whatever you wanna ask, and I'm just supposed to—I don't even know what—sit here and just submit to whatever you wanna ask whenever you wanna ask it?! It's fuckin' bullshit!

THERESE MARIE Danny—

DANNY No! No! You asked your questions, now let me ask mine, 'cuz I only got one: How come I can't go *anywhere* without you ending up in a hospital somewhere and I gotta come back and fuckin' tend to it?! Forget about fun shit, forget about fuckin' career shit—how come I can't go to fuckin' *rehab* to try to *save my fuckin' life* without you going off the deep end and trying to—I don't know what—and then you end up here, and I gotta deal with it, and deal with fuckin' *you* when all I should be truly trying to deal with right now is fuckin' *me*?! And you can say "Oh, honey, I want you to be free, Danny" all you want, but the fact is, you want me to be free only to the degree that it doesn't adversely affect you!

THERESE MARIE Why do you think I did what I did if it wasn't to let you and Justina be free?! I pray every night for God to take me, and the only reason I don't commit suicide is because the Church forbids it—and if I took my own life I wouldn't be able to see the three of you in heaven!

DANNY Mom, you don't think escaping the house and wheeling yourself to the fuckin' Cloisters in the dead of winter in a fuckin' nightgown doesn't qualify as a suicide attempt?

THERESE MARIE I was only thinking of you! I was thinking of you!

Beat.

DANNY You know what's really fucked up, Mom? What's really fucked up . . . is the fact that I actually believe you . . . and what's even more fucked up than that is the fact that you're broken beyond repair and I still believe I have no right to anything past failed expectations and self-medication unless I can fix you—'cuz it's not okay to pass you by . . .

FRANCIS JAMES *appears and begins signing to her. He signs silently throughout the following.*

THERESE MARIE Oh. Poppa!

DANNY What?

FRANCIS JAMES When you were born, Therese, everyone said, "What will you do now, Francis? You're deaf. Sarah's deaf. How will you hear your baby girl at night when she cries?"

DANNY Ma, what're you doing?

THERESE MARIE (*to* DANNY) Poppa's telling me a story from when I was born. (*to* FRANCIS JAMES) Yes, Poppa! . . . (*to* DANNY) When I was born, everybody told him and my mother, "You're deaf! How will you hear your baby girl at night when she cries?" (to FRANCIS JAMES) Yes, Poppa!

DANNY Mom?!

FRANCIS JAMES Your uncle Barney thought he and Aunt Kitty should raise you.

THERESE MARIE They all thought that Uncle Barney and Aunt Kitty should raise me, Danny. (*to* FRANCIS JAMES) I know, Poppa. But you wouldn't let that happen.

FRANCIS JAMES I told your mother, "We are her parents and we will solve the problem."

THERESE MARIE He told my mother, "We are her parents and we will solve the problem."

DANNY Mom, what the fuck?

FRANCIS JAMES We tied a string to my foot, and we put the string out the window down to Mrs. Ambersini's kitchen window downstairs, and whenever you cried at night, Mrs. Ambersini would just pull the string and jerk my foot, and then we'd wake up and know you needed us.

THERESE MARIE Yes, Poppa. He tied a string to his foot—yes, yes—and he put the string out the window down to Mrs. Ambersini's kitchen window downstairs, and when I cried at night, Mrs. Ambersini would pull the string and jerk his foot to wake him up. Can you imagine that? And that's how he knew if I needed him!

FRANCIS JAMES We solved the problem, didn't we?

THERESE MARIE You solved the problem, Poppa, you did.

FRANCIS JAMES *disappears.*

DANNY Mom? Mom!

ESPINOSA *enters.*

ESPINOSA *Mami*—you see *puto*?

THERESE MARIE Oh, hello! Oh! Have you met my son? Mr. Espinosa, this is Danny. He used to be a very well-known writer. *The New York Times* called him "a bright light on the horizon"!

ESPINOSA "Bright light." Berry good, berry nice. (*to* THERESE MARIE) So, *mami: puto*, you see him?

THERESE MARIE Mr. Puto? Uh. He was here. Poor man: he's like white bread soaked in milk. I don't know. Did he go home?

ESPINOSA The coat is here. The umbrella is here. The hat is here. But the *puto*? He no here . . . Okay, I go. Chessmens coming, *mami*!

DANNY Wait.

THERESE MARIE Thank you, Mr. Espinosa.

ESPINOSA (*to* DANNY) Your *mami*—nobody like her! Nobody! *Una santa enviada del cielo! My* mother? Forgetaboutit. *Pafuera!* Dump her in the garbage! But *your* mother? You got the blessing, *papi.*

DANNY Listen, she just like, bugged out. Seeing things.

ESPINOSA Morphine.

DANNY But she's on morphine all the time.

ESPINOSA No. She came here with a morphine pump in her body, *pero* they hadda take it out. So she withdrawing. We putting the morphine back in, but slowly, otherwise— no good. That's why she talking with Frank Sinatra. (*to* THERESE MARIE) *Mami,* how's Frank Sinatra today, good?

THERESE MARIE Oh, you smart aleck.

ESPINOSA (*to* DANNY) You see? Okay.

He exits. Beat.

THERESE MARIE He's such a lovely boy.

DANNY Mom—

THERESE MARIE —Apparently, his mother is a very troubled woman, you know, disturbed, poor thing, and his brother just got deported for, well, mixing with the wrong crowd. I think he's very lonesome, Danny, but you would never know it. So full of the devil. Just lovely. He's studying for his certificate in air-conditioning and refrigeration.

DANNY That's great, Mom.

THERESE MARIE Danny?

DANNY Yeah?

THERESE MARIE Is there any scotch?

DANNY I'm an alcoholic, Ma.

THERESE MARIE And you're getting help, and I'm very proud—

DANNY Then why would you be asking me for scotch?

THERESE MARIE Well . . . Is there any?

DANNY See, Ma, this is what I'm talking about!

THERESE MARIE What?

DANNY Do you honestly fail to see the fuckin' whaddyacallit—the fuckin' discrepancy—between what a normal person wouldn't ask her son for—and what you just did?

THERESE MARIE What did I do?

DANNY There's a fuckin' discrepancy here, Mom!

THERESE MARIE Oh, discrepancy horse manure!

DANNY Would you give your father a drink if he asked for one?

THERESE MARIE That's silly—there's a big difference between you and my father!

DANNY Yeah?! And what exactly is the difference?

THERESE MARIE Honey, I used to give money to the bums on the street, and people would say, What are you doing that for, they're just going to buy a bottle. And I would say, Well, maybe that's what they need!

DANNY But that's not what I asked you!

THERESE MARIE Frank Sinatra said, "Whatever gets you through the night"!

DANNY Mom, you wanna fuckin' bottle, I'll buy you a fuckin' bottle!

THERESE MARIE You make me sound like some skid-row bum! I'm in *pain*, Danny, and I wish to heavens I was dead—and the scotch doesn't cure the pain, it just flattens it out a little! Jesus, Mary, and Joseph—you'd think I was asking for the moon!!

DANNY I'm gonna go outside and buy you a fuckin' case!

THERESE MARIE Oh, don't buy me anything with that nasty rotten temper of yours! You should do what Harry Truman did!

DANNY Drop a bomb on Nagasaki?!

THERESE MARIE No, jackass, not drop a bomb on Nagasaki! When Harry Truman got good and angry, instead of blowing up, he'd write it in a letter, then put it in his desk and never mail it. It was a very good technique!

DANNY Harry Truman, huh?

THERESE MARIE Of course, poor President Truman, after he died they found the letters when they moved his desk to the Truman Library, and they made them available for public viewing, so it kind of defeated the purpose, but—

DANNY —That's a lovely story, Mom. I'm gonna go out and shoot myself in the head, I'll be right back.

THERESE MARIE . . . Are you going to bring the scotch?

Beat. DANNY *regards her. A face-off.*

DANNY Ma, remember that time when you were heavier and I was younger, and you had that heart thing, and we made that deal that I'd quit smoking if you stopped eating butter?

THERESE MARIE . . . Oh, you miserable wretch, yes! I didn't eat butter for *two months* before I figured out that you'd never quit smoking in the first place!

DANNY Right. What made you willing to give up the butter?

THERESE MARIE You know damn well why I gave it up. My father, my mother, my sister—they all died from *smoking.* I don't want that for you.

DANNY Right. You were my mom back then . . . I'll go get the scotch.

He exits. Lights fade.

DAVID HALZIG *stands on the roof near the ledge, staring out at the city. He is crying.*

ESPINOSA *enters.* DAVID HALZIG *hides his tears by keeping his back to* ESPINOSA.

ESPINOSA *Puto!* This is the roof! "Nobody no people" supposed to be on the roof without you supposed to ax somebody first! Okay?

DAVID HALZIG Oh.

ESPINOSA "Oh," what?! What that means, "Oh"?

DAVID HALZIG I'm sorry.

ESPINOSA You lucky I like you, *puto.* Otherwise you would be punished, you better believe it.

DAVID HALZIG I believe it.

ESPINOSA It's not my job to track down lost *putos*, okay?

DAVID HALZIG Yes.

ESPINOSA Okay. Move back from the ledge, otherwise maybe a pigeon gonna knock you over and then no more *puto.*

DAVID HALZIG Sorry.

ESPINOSA If you fall off the roof, your *mami* gonna get bad dreams, *puto*, believe me. And then Nuestra Señora del Altagracia gonna put *una maldición* on your head and you gonna turn into a chicken with one hoof and with no fuckin' beak! You want to have no fuckin' beak?

DAVID HALZIG No.

ESPINOSA *lights a cigarette.*

ESPINOSA Anyway . . . Nice night. Smart of you to get
some air.

Pause.

DAVID HALZIG I'm sad, Mr. Espinosa. And I don't know what
to do.

ESPINOSA I'm sad too, *puto*. And I don't know what to do
either. Okay?

DAVID HALZIG They took Mom up to the ICU. I don't think
she's coming back.

ESPINOSA *Puto*, do you know what ICU stands for?

DAVID HALZIG Intensive Care Unit.

ESPINOSA Yes. But do you know what it *also* stands for?

DAVID HALZIG It stands for Intensive Care Unit. That's what
it stands for. Intensive Care.

ESPINOSA That's correct. But, ICU, *puto*, also stands for—

DAVID HALZIG That's what it stands for, Mr. Espinosa. It
doesn't stand for anything else.

ESPINOSA Okay fine, then. ICU does not stand for "I
challenge you."

DAVID HALZIG "I challenge you"?

ESPINOSA Das right, *puto*. A lot of visitors, they not like you.
ICU say, "I challenge you." They say, "*Aye, papi*, boohoo,
I surrender." You know what I mean? When ICU say, "I
challenge you," you gotta say, "Fuck you, ICU. I see you
too! And I challenge *you*." You see?

DAVID HALZIG I. Yes. I do.

ESPINOSA . . . Okay. Now. Learn something else. Right here is where?

DAVID HALZIG The roof?

ESPINOSA No. Look out there. Right here is Walton Avenue, okay? Walton. You see the bodega?

DAVID HALZIG I think so.

ESPINOSA Good. Where we are now, Walton Avenue. Over there, Grand Concourse. But over *there*—you see dat?

DAVID HALZIG What?

ESPINOSA Dat!

DAVID HALZIG Um . . .

ESPINOSA Dat, *puto*, dat! You don't see that?!

DAVID HALZIG I think so.

ESPINOSA Educate you mind, *puto*. Dat's Yanqui Stadium! 880 River Avenue. You know who plays there?

DAVID HALZIG The Yankees?

ESPINOSA Robinson Canó! You know Robinson Canó?

DAVID HALZIG Um . . .

ESPINOSA Robinson Canó! Best second base in *béisbol*! From my people. Robinson Canó! "Get to know Ca-nó," okay?!

DAVID HALZIG Okay.

ESPINOSA And now, *puto*, okay: if you looky way over *there*—

DAVID HALZIG Where?

ESPINOSA Over there, *puto*—

DAVID HALZIG Over there where?

ESPINOSA Over there so far you can't see it but it's fuckin' there, *puto*! Over *there*, over *there*, that's where plays who?

DAVID HALZIG Uh . . . the Giants?

ESPINOSA The Giants?!

DAVID HALZIG The Giants, right? Football?

ESPINOSA The Giants?! Mothahfuckah, you fly planes? You a fuckin' pilot?

DAVID HALZIG No.

ESPINOSA Das good, 'cuz you don't know where nothing is! How you go through life not knowing where nothing is? Someday, someone gonna take you to somewhere you don't wanna go, but you're no gonna know, 'cuz you don't know nothing about where nothing is, okay?! Now, *puto*, look with your *eyes*: over there across the fuckin' river plays the Giants, right here plays Yankees, but over *there*—over *there, puto*—plays *who*??

DAVID HALZIG Um . . .

ESPINOSA *Who*?!

DAVID HALZIG Um . . . Pedro?

ESPINOSA Das right! Das the mothahfuckah who's playing over there! Fuckin' Pedro! Berry good! You see? Now you know some things.

DAVID HALZIG . . . I knew some things before.

ESPINOSA Okay, Professor, you know a lot of things, okay? Now move your ass downstairs, *puto*, I gotta lock up.

DAVID HALZIG But I'd like to stay here.

ESPINOSA Yeah, and I'd like to make fuckin' *puñeta* in Dr. Shankar's soup—you know Dr. Shankar, bald mothahfuckah—but that's not gonna happen either, okay? So stop playing me, *puto*. Move your ass. Les go!

DAVID HALZIG *begins to exit—*

ESPINOSA And *puto*?

DAVID HALZIG Yes?

ESPINOSA Nobody going nowhere no time soon, okay? Now go back down there and don't fuck around. Okay, *puto*?

DAVID HALZIG Yes.

ESPINOSA Good. And *puto*, ICU also mean *one* more thing.

DAVID HALZIG What?

ESPINOSA ICU up here again—kapow! Okay, my friend?

DAVID HALZIG Yes, Mr. Espinosa.

ESPINOSA Good. Berry good.

DAVID HALZIG *exits.* ESPINOSA *tosses his cigarette.*

ESPINOSA Fuckin' *puto* . . .

SCENE 3 • THE HOSPITAL ROOM

THERESE MARIE *is in a wheelchair, a small suitcase by her side. She is doing a crossword. She's in pain from the sitting.*

JUSTINA *is standing and texting on her BlackBerry, visibly on edge.*

MAGNOLIA *enters in street clothes. As always, she looks very proper.*

MAGNOLIA Hello, Terry. Going home today, I see.

THERESE MARIE Oh, hello.

MAGNOLIA You don't recognize me? What's the matter with you, girl! It's Magnolia.

THERESE MARIE Magnolia, of course. I must be batty!

MAGNOLIA No no, I'm not in uniform. I have to go down to my daughter's school.

THERESE MARIE Oh, how nice.

MAGNOLIA No. Not nice. She making trouble there. I'm paying top dollar for that school and she want to go an' act the fool, can you imagine?

THERESE MARIE Well, you look lovely. Justina? . . . Justina! I'd like you to meet my "drill sergeant." This is Miss Magnolia.

JUSTINA Hello. My mother speaks so highly of you.

MAGNOLIA Stop lying!

MAGNOLIA *laughs heartily. Which makes* THERESE MARIE *laugh as well.*

THERESE MARIE (*re:* MAGNOLIA) She's a tough SOB!

JUSTINA Anyway, this is a little something for you.

MAGNOLIA I can't take that.

JUSTINA Take it. Please. I insist.

MAGNOLIA Thank you.

JUSTINA And can you give this one to . . . Mr. Espinosa?

MAGNOLIA That loggaheaded hooligan?! Your mother's too nice. (*to* THERESE MARIE) Thank you, Terry.

JUSTINA Do you by any chance know where the doctor is? He was supposed to be here an hour and forty-five minutes ago, and we're waiting to go to the nursing home.

MAGNOLIA Nursing home? . . . Which nursing home you going?

THERESE MARIE We're waiting for an opening.

MAGNOLIA (*to* JUSTINA) Listen now: When you get there, put the family pictures by the bedside—let them people remember they're tending to a person. Really, all them places not too bad, but if you have a choice, go to the Jewish . . .

JUSTINA Thank you.

MAGNOLIA Terry, you gonna be strong for me?

THERESE MARIE Give me your hand.

MAGNOLIA Yes, dear.

THERESE MARIE There are saints walking this earth, Magnolia. I believe that strongly. I may be old and dopey, but I don't miss a trick, honey. You are a saint, and I thank you.

MAGNOLIA Listen to you—politician!

THERESE MARIE You're lovely. And a saint.

MAGNOLIA Thank you. God bless.

MAGNOLIA *exits.*

JUSTINA . . . Master of hyperbole, Mommy.

JUSTINA *resumes texting.*

THERESE MARIE It's not hyperbole!

JUSTINA Mommy: you actually believe that woman is a *saint*? That one day she'll be canonized by a pope and we'll all be celebrating the Feast of Saint Magnolia Day on the second Sunday of whatever?

THERESE MARIE Oh, dry up.

JUSTINA I'm not making fun of you. It's actually a good quality to have. People love you, Mom.

THERESE MARIE Oh, honey—I'm the least of His creatures.

JUSTINA Right. I forgot: you, Hitler, and the shah of Iran.

THERESE MARIE . . . Where's Danny?

JUSTINA He went to put that little girl on the Amtrak.

THERESE MARIE She's going home?

JUSTINA Home. Rehab. Amsterdam. Who knows. He's a magnet for strays—just like someone else I know.

THERESE MARIE Oh, honey—"Open door, open heart."

JUSTINA "Open smelling salts, insert face"—that's a lot more like it.

THERESE MARIE Honey—

JUSTINA —I don't want to talk about it.

THERESE MARIE . . . Tell me about Chicago again.

JUSTINA (*a warning*) Mom . . .

THERESE MARIE I saw Tallulah Bankhead in a touring show in Chicago once, a revival of Thornton Wilder, I think it was—and then, afterward, she was at the same nightclub as us, and boy could she throw it back! Oh, she was a wild one. But what an actress!

DR. SHANKAR *enters with a clipboard of* THERESE MARIE'*s paperwork.*

JUSTINA Oh. Hello.

DR. SHANKAR Dr. Shankar. We spoke on the phone.

JUSTINA Yes.

DR. SHANKAR Hello, Terry.

THERESE MARIE Oh, hello, Dr. Shank. Justina, did you meet Dr. Shank?

JUSTINA About two seconds ago, Mom, and his name's Shankar.

THERESE MARIE Yes. That's what I said.

DR. SHANKAR So, I spoke with the staff gerontologist and she will be faxing some recommendations to the nursing home with regard to your mother's condition.

THERESE MARIE Excuse me, may I be included in this?

JUSTINA Mom—no one's trying to exclude you—

THERESE MARIE —I would like to know—

JUSTINA —Mom! I'm trying to collect information, okay? I love you, now back off! (*to* SHANKAR) I'm sorry.

DR. SHANKAR Yes, anyway, the—

THERESE MARIE Like I'm not even here . . . !

JUSTINA Mom.

DR. SHANKAR I can see I'm not the only one.

JUSTINA Excuse me?

DR. SHANKAR Now, Terry, we've found a nice place for you. It's not far from where you live.

JUSTINA Is it Jewish?

DR. SHANKAR No, but it's close to the family address.

JUSTINA We want the Jewish one.

THERESE MARIE Oh, honey, I don't want Danny having to travel far—

JUSTINA He can take a subway. (*to* SHANKAR) We'd like the Jewish one, please.

DR. SHANKAR I'll have to check if it's still available.

JUSTINA I'd appreciate it, thank you—because that's the one we would have chosen if we had been presented with an option.

DR. SHANKAR I'll do that then. Now, the social worker has some recommendations as well—

JUSTINA Could you do it now? My understanding is that rooms go quickly.

DR. SHANKAR . . . I'll be back.

JUSTINA Thank you very much, Doctor.

DR. SHANKAR *exits.*

THERESE MARIE Good for you, kiddo! That sonuvabitch.

JUSTINA He's just doing his job, Mom. Have you seen this place? It's like a VA hospital from the seventies. Next time you run away from home, head southeast toward NYU or Lenox Hill.

THERESE MARIE . . . Well, I won't be going home ever again, so you needn't worry.

JUSTINA Mom!

THERESE MARIE No, no, I'm not complaining, honey—that's life! People live too long nowadays anyway—all this science—and for what?! I wish they had never resuscitated me. I was happy to go!

JUSTINA Well, we're glad you're here, Mom—so can we please not talk about this?

THERESE MARIE Your father's coronary was the best thing that ever happened to him, and that's the first thing I'll tell him after I meet my maker!

JUSTINA Mom—

THERESE MARIE I'm like a noose around Danny's neck—and thank God you're off to Chicago!

JUSTINA I'm not "off to Chicago," Mom! My new company is *based* in Chicago. I'll be there one weekend a month!

THERESE MARIE You oughta run while the getting's good!

JUSTINA You're the one who "ran," Mom, not me!

THERESE MARIE Oh, you're gonna hold on to that one like a miser clinging to his silk purse, aren't you?! Well, at least you're not the one being consigned to the trash heap like a broken-down jalopy! And I'll tell you something else: I don't want any of the neighbors to know I'm in a nursing home—tell them I'm in the hospital or that I just dropped dead!

JUSTINA Oh my God . . . Number one: You're the one who insisted on going to a nursing home. Not me. I just happen to strenuously agree. Number two: I'm going to have to take out a loan to pay for it until your Medicaid comes through, which, I'm the one doing all that incredibly time-consuming paperwork—not Danny and not you. And number three: If this is hard for you, which I'm sure that it is . . . you might also take into consideration . . . that it's fuckin' really, really hard for me too! (*Breaks down.*)

THERESE MARIE Oh, honey, I'm sorry—please, oh, I feel awful, awful—

JUSTINA Yeah, well, other people feel awful too!

THERESE MARIE . . . I . . . I didn't know you felt this way.

JUSTINA You didn't know I felt this way?! (*Collects herself.*) You know what, I'm not going to have this conversation, because somebody in this family needs to keep it together right now, and it's not going to be Danny and it's not going to be you. So the two of you can just go off and be with the rest of the wounded martyrs and the selfless saints while I play my usual role of the cold, bitchy, hysterical, insensitive one—also known as the only one who actually gets things done! You hurt me so much, Mommy! You didn't know that I *felt* this way? Well, maybe if you had an ounce of self-esteem or self-worth, if you didn't let people walk all over you, if you didn't always forgive to your own detriment, and think of everyone else but yourself—oh, what's the use!

THERESE MARIE I love you, Justina.

JUSTINA I don't doubt that, Mommy. That's not the issue. I mean we used to joke about Daddy having no hobbies, but at least he had the OTB, and at least his lack of emotion allowed for some space to fuckin' breathe.

THERESE MARIE . . . I feel you don't understand me at all. Like I'm nothing. Like I've done nothing.

JUSTINA Mom, I thank you all the time for what you've given me genetically, and in terms of upbringing and values, and inspiration. You did a lot.

THERESE MARIE Not enough. I failed miserably—miserably!

JUSTINA There's just no way to make this not all about you, is there?

THERESE MARIE I just want to say . . . that the doctors said I was crazy to risk having another child—crazy—that I'd die, or that you could turn out a mongoloid—

JUSTINA —Mom: Danny moved in with you the day Daddy died, and in all that time, you never ran away from home on a suicidal death mission. I'm there with you for three days—three days, Mom, and you know how I am—and you wheel yourself out of my life while I'm out buying a carton of milk and some graham crackers. Does it penetrate your brain how that might make me feel? Did you take into account the psychic damage you would have inflicted had you died before we found you? That my last words to my mother would have been "Go fuck yourself, I hope you die"?! . . . And is it possible, Mom, that what you did actually had more to do with *narcissism* and *passive aggression* than it did with being a martyr and "wanting your children to be free"?! Did you ever think of that?!

Beat.

THERESE MARIE Justina—

DANNY *enters with a liter of Johnnie Walker in a paper bag.*

DANNY Hey.

Beat.

DANNY What's going on?
JUSTINA . . . That is not a bottle of liquor in your hand!
DANNY Uh, no, it's not.
JUSTINA Give it to me.

She takes the bottle, glares at DANNY, inspects it, opens it, takes a massive swig, closes the cap, puts it back in the bag, and puts it in her purse.

JUSTINA Mom, wipe off your face so I can put on your makeup.

DANNY Brought you some mints, Mom.

DR. SHANKAR *enters.*

DR. SHANKAR Okay, yes. Manhattan Jewish Home and Hospital, 120 West 106th Street. There's an ambulette coming to get you in maybe fifteen minutes.

JUSTINA Thank you, Doctor.

DR. SHANKAR Now to the paperwork—

JUSTINA —No really, thank you.

DR. SHANKAR We do our best.

DANNY "Manhattan Jewish" what?

DR. SHANKAR This is the insurance form. And this one is to be given to the social worker upon arrival—

DANNY Hey. I asked a question. Manhattan Jewish what?

THERESE MARIE Honey, it's for the best—

JUSTINA Mommy's going to a nursing home. The doctor recommends it. It's been decided.

DR. SHANKAR This form is to be filled out and brought to Admissions—

DANNY Whaddya mean, "It's been decided"? Who decided, and how was anything decided without me?

DR. SHANKAR Really, sir, it's for the best—

DANNY —I'm sorry but I wasn't speaking to you—

JUSTINA Danny, don't start!

DANNY Don't start what?! What the fuck is going on here?

THERESE MARIE Honey, I want to go—it's where I want to go.

DANNY Mom, you've been in those places before, after surgeries—and you were suicidal!

JUSTINA Danny—

DANNY —Don't fuckin' "Danny" me like I'm a little fuckin' kid!

JUSTINA Then stop acting like a little kid! Mommy flatlined in here, she's not well, and she needs fast access to medical attention if necessary. Tell him!

DR. SHANKAR It's true.

JUSTINA Besides that, she needs care—care you cannot provide!

DANNY She was fine before!

JUSTINA This isn't before, this is now! Tell him!

DR. SHANKAR It would be advisable.

DANNY Well, is it just "advisable" that she go, or is it mandatory?

JUSTINA You can visit her whenever you want!

DANNY Well, maybe I don't wanna spend ten hours a day in a fuckin' nursing home—

THERESE MARIE Really, Danny, you don't have to come at all.

JUSTINA Mom! Shut up!

DR. SHANKAR I'll leave you to decide.

JUSTINA No. Please. One minute. (*re:* DANNY) He has a drinking problem, a drug problem, and he's clinically depressed. He was in a rehab getting help before all this happened. I bought him a new laptop last Christmas, and he hasn't even taken it out of the box! The apartment is a mess. He feeds her cookies, ice cream, and scotch. I'm afraid he's going to die soon if he doesn't wake up and smell the fuckin' coffee. He needs to focus on himself,

Doctor—not taking care of someone else—who he can't care for properly in the first place! His heart's in the right place, but his head is up his ass! Now: your comments, please . . .

Beat.

DR. SHANKAR (*to* DANNY) May I address you?

DANNY Yeah.

DR. SHANKAR First: I sympathize. I come from a close-knit family. And a culture that puts family number one. Okay?

DANNY Yes.

DR. SHANKAR Your intentions are honorable.

DANNY Look, Doctor—

JUSTINA Let him finish!

DR. SHANKAR (*to* JUSTINA) Please. (*to* DANNY) You have a full plate. Very full. If I was my grandfather, I'd be saying to you: The Great Tiger cannot swim in the bay after a large supper, and the Bronzed Cow cannot graze . . .

JUSTINA He can't graze, Danny—and neither can you!

DR. SHANKAR (*to* JUSTINA) Please. (*to* DANNY) Try the nursing home. Deal with your issues. And then—bring her back home if you like.

THERESE MARIE That makes a lot of sense, honey.

JUSTINA Thank you, Doctor.

All eyes on DANNY.

DANNY . . . Is it "advisable" or "mandatory"? Which one?

JUSTINA Danny—

DANNY Which one?

DR. SHANKAR . . . Advisable.

DANNY Thank you. C'mon, Mom, we're going home.

JUSTINA We've already filled out the paperwork!

DANNY What paperwork?

He grabs the paperwork out of DR. SHANKAR*'s hands and rips it up piece by piece in an incredibly out-of-control and violent fashion.*

JUSTINA You're a fuckin' maniac!

THERESE MARIE Danny, calm down!

DR. SHANKAR I'm getting Espinosa.

DR. SHANKAR *exits.* DANNY *subdues himself.*

Pause.

JUSTINA . . . You're such a fuckin' asshole, Danny.

THERESE MARIE *is weeping—a reaction to the violence.*

DANNY (*to* JUSTINA) We'll get a home attendant. Maybe a woman to live with us like Mrs. Toledo. I'll deal with my shit. But she is not going to a nursing home.

Beat.

JUSTINA (*to* DANNY) I tried to help you. (to THERESE MARIE) I tried to help you too.

JUSTINA *gathers her things.*

JUSTINA I'll send a fuckin' check. (*Exits.*)

DANNY . . . Mom?

THERESE MARIE I'm so upset.

DANNY Mom.

THERESE MARIE I caused a rift between you two—I wish I were dead.

DANNY Mom. Mom, look at me.

DANNY *goes to her. Comforts her.*

DANNY Justina will be fine. It'll be fine.

THERESE MARIE I love her so much, Danny.

DANNY I love her too.

THERESE MARIE I want to go to the nursing home.

DANNY I'm not letting you die in a nursing home, Mom. Would you put me in a nursing home?

THERESE MARIE I love you so much, Danny.

DANNY Now listen. We're gonna go home. And you're gonna have your books and your newspapers and your view of the river and your radio and whatever else you want. I'm going to quit drinking. And I'm going to buy you an easel so you can paint—remember how you used to like to paint?

THERESE MARIE It was chicken scratch.

DANNY Well then, you'll make some new chicken scratch.

THERESE MARIE Will you write, Danny? I'd be so happy if you wrote.

DANNY Yeah, Mom, I'll write.

THERESE MARIE But not about me.

DANNY I won't write about you, don't worry.

THERESE MARIE After I'm gone. After I'm gone, open season.

DANNY Okay . . . And Mom—everything will be okay, okay?

ESPINOSA *enters.*

ESPINOSA Everything all right in here?

DANNY It's fine. Everything is fine.

Lights fade.

SCENE 4

The apartment, in the living room, by the window, overlooking the Hudson River. Glenn Miller, or the like, plays.

DANNY The last time I saw my mom was in the living room of our old rent-controlled apartment on Riverside Drive.

Lights reveal THERESE MARIE *in her wheelchair upstage. Her handheld radio plays Glenn Miller.*

THERESE MARIE Wheel me to the window, would you, Danny?

DANNY Sure, Mom. Hold these.

He hands her a glass of scotch and a forty.

THERESE MARIE Oh, my, "double-fisted," isn't that what they say?

DANNY That's what they say, Mom, yup . . . Here we are.

THERESE MARIE Thank you, honey.

She stares out at the river, sipping her scotch. DANNY *lingers, sips his forty.*

THERESE MARIE I'm okay, Danny. Go on and watch your
program. I'll turn off my radio so it doesn't disturb you.

DANNY Okay.

DANNY *turns to leave her. He starts walking away, then stops and regards her.*

Beat.

DANNY *pulls up a chair and sits next to her. She pats his hand and continues staring out.*

Beat.

THERESE MARIE . . . I love the tugboats.

DANNY . . . I know you do.

THERESE MARIE All those big important ships going to big
important places—halfway around the world and back
again—but without the tugboat? They're nothing.
Useless. It's that little tugboat that lights the way and
shoulders the load and carries them "safe to sea."

DANNY That's very poetic, Mom.

THERESE MARIE Oh, I'm no poet.

DANNY Of course not. Not you.

THERESE MARIE Nature is a poet, Danny. God is a poet. My son is a poet.

DANNY I'm not a poet, Mom.

THERESE MARIE Oh yes you are. Yes you are. *"Le gâteau de la plume!"*—that's my son!

DANNY . . . "The cake of the feather," Mom?? . . .

THERESE MARIE Oh, you know what I mean.

DANNY (*mimicking her*) Oh, *oui, oui!* *"Le gâteau de la plume!"*

THERESE MARIE (*laughing*) Oh, honey—

DANNY And you said it so confidently—like you were Napoleon leading the troops into battle: "*Le gâteau de la plume*, gentlemen"! *"Le gâteau de la plume!!"*

THERESE MARIE Cadeau! Okay, big shot? You have *"le cadeau de la plume"*—the gift of the pen!

DANNY Oh yeah?

THERESE MARIE That's right, kiddo.

DANNY Well, can I get the gift of the Lotto jackpot instead?

THERESE MARIE Honey, that is a Lotto jackpot. You have no idea. Your grandfather had it. He always said, "You can get anything you want in this world with a letter"—that's how he wooed my mother.

DANNY That turned out well.

THERESE MARIE I wouldn't be here today if he hadn't written those letters—and neither would you!

DANNY Okay, okay . . . How about you tell me more about them tugboats.

THERESE MARIE . . . My father was a kind, decent man with a brilliant, brilliant mind, Danny. Not "bright"—brilliant.

DANNY Yes, Mom: brilliant and kind.

THERESE MARIE You have no idea his acts of kindness. You have no idea.

DANNY I got it, Mom: "Fists of Fury had a heart of gold," okay? Can we move on?

THERESE MARIE Oh, you're just so smart, aren't you? Go watch your program, Danny. Really, I was enjoying the calm and quiet.

DANNY So I ruined the calm and quiet . . .

THERESE MARIE I don't want to argue with you. Just go.

DANNY I was just sitting here, Mom.

THERESE MARIE Sitting here, yes—with your sarcasm lying in wait, like a thief in the night.

DANNY I was joking.

THERESE MARIE "The tearing of the flesh"—that's what sarcasm is, Danny! Tearing! From the Latin. That's not humor. That's viciousness. Vicious.

DANNY I'm sorry.

THERESE MARIE Go away, Danny, my head is pounding.

DANNY I'm sorry, Mom.

THERESE MARIE When I first got out of the hospital after ten years in a hospital bed, ten years of surgeries, and pain, and pain, and boredom—stultifying boredom—and people worried about me all the time—"Oh, Terry," "Poor Terry"—and my poor parents trekking out to East Orange every Sunday—every Sunday, Danny, my father never missed a Sunday—with newspapers and books for me, anything they could get their hands on—magazines, brochures, batteries for my little radio, hot cross buns at Eastertime—oh, it was awful—awful—what they went through . . . And when I got home, I was just so sick of being looked out for—"Oh, is she okay?"—every sigh or moan a cause for concern—I'd keep my face as pain-free as I could when I walked around the house so I wouldn't worry my parents—and it was just too much, and I decided that I needed to get away for a few days—and now, I had never been farther than Aunt Grace's house in Philadelphia—but I put my mind to it, I had seen a picture book of Nantucket, and I decided: "I don't know why or how—but I'm going there." And at Sunday dinner, I told my family, "I'm going to Nantucket." And you should have heard the uproar: "Oh no, you can't go," "What if you get hurt?" "You've just been in bed for ten years," and then—"Well, why don't you take somebody with you?" And I said, "No. Maybe I'll get to Grand Central and have to turn right back around, but I'm going on my own." And again, the uproar: "You can't go," "Please don't," "We forbid it"—but then—my father—God love him—he banged the table, like this— *bang!* And then he signed to everyone—"No. No. She's right. She's had enough of us. She's had *enough*. She needs to go." . . . I'll love him forever for that. He knew. And he knew me. And of course he was terrified, but he let me go. Because he knew. He *knew!*

DANNY   Okay, Mom, I'm totally with you on the "he knew" thing, and I'm also with you on the whole emotional drama of it all, which, you've told me this story a million times and it still makes me cry—

THERESE MARIE   He understood me—

DANNY   —And that he understood you—

THERESE MARIE   —It meant everything—

DANNY —"Everything," I know, and please trust me when I say I don't mean to diminish—

THERESE MARIE What it took for him to say that—

DANNY —I'm sure it took a lot—

THERESE MARIE —And how!

DANNY But for one thing, Mom—you were thirty years old at that time. And secondly: if it wasn't for your father, you wouldn't have had to spend ten years in the fuckin' hospital in the first place.

THERESE MARIE That's not true!

DANNY It's not?

THERESE MARIE Danny, I rue the day I ever told you anything about my childhood.

DANNY Well, "rue" away all you want, Mom, but you did tell me.

THERESE MARIE I speak to you about something *private*, I take you into my confidence in a moment of ungrateful, disloyal weakness on my part—because I have no one else to speak to—and you just go off and run with it and turn my father into a monster!

DANNY I'm not saying he was a monster.

THERESE MARIE You have no idea what a good man he was!

DANNY I'm not saying he wasn't a good man. I'm saying that he cost you ten years in a hospital bed, Mom, on top of all the other stuff, and that's a fuckin' fact.

THERESE MARIE That's not what happened!

DANNY Mom, I can't stop you from embellishing the past, but you can't *rewrite* it—

THERESE MARIE —Oh, "rewrite it" my foot!—

DANNY You broke your back when you were eighteen under mysterious circumstances—

THERESE MARIE —There was nothing mysterious about it! It was an after-school class in the gymnasium, they were toughening the boys up for the war, and I signed up because I wanted to lose weight!

DANNY Okay, fine. And what happened next?

THERESE MARIE Honey, this is ancient history!

DANNY Mom: the Peloponnesian War is ancient history. The fall of fuckin' Rome, okay, that's ancient history. This shit is not ancient history—this is fuckin' CNN "up to the minute" Wolf Blitzer, fuckin' Anderson fuckin' Cooper shit, okay? This is the air we breathe.

THERESE MARIE Your cigarette smoke is the air I breathe, Danny—and I cry myself to sleep because it's killing you!

DANNY And we'll have plenty of time to endlessly harp on *that* after we're done with *this*: You broke your back, Mom. You went to some hospital in North Arlington—

THERESE MARIE Newark.

DANNY Okay, Newark—

THERESE MARIE The Saint James Roman Catholic Orphan Asylum and Hospital in Newark, New Jersey—

DANNY Okay.

THERESE MARIE A lovely place. They were the only ones out of all of them who knew their asses from their elbows.

DANNY And they fixed you up there, right?

THERESE MARIE Oh, honey, the past is the past—

DANNY Did they fix you up there or not, Mom?!

THERESE MARIE Yes! They fixed me up! It took several months, I had just started college—and Poppa was bringing me

the books and the assignments so I wouldn't fall behind—
Are you happy? You're like a dog with a bone!

DANNY And then what happened?

THERESE MARIE You think you know what happened anyway,
so why do you insist on beating it out of me?

DANNY Okay: You got home. You were recuperating. Sitting,
resting, walking—following the doctor's orders—

THERESE MARIE The doctor said it was a miracle: it was
"experimental" surgery—I was a test case.

DANNY I know you were. And you were keeping up with
your studies from home, weren't you?

THERESE MARIE (*dismissively*) Oh, I loved to study—it was an
escape.

DANNY And then what happened?

THERESE MARIE Honey, you're a bore!

DANNY What happened next, Mom?

THERESE MARIE Oh, stick a sock in it, Clarence Darrow—
you're a bore, bore, bore!

DANNY The doorbell rang, didn't it?

THERESE MARIE I'd like another scotch, please.

DANNY You've already had two, Mom, and you're floating
on morphine on top of it.

THERESE MARIE And what are you floating on, Danny—
because don't think I don't know.

DANNY The doorbell rang—

THERESE MARIE I want another scotch.

DANNY Finish the story and I'll give you one.

THERESE MARIE Oh, don't you dare! Don't you dare treat me
like some child! This is my house and my scotch, and I
want some now!

DANNY Well, I'll tell you what, Mom: the scotch is right
    behind you in the pocket on the back of your wheelchair,
    and if your father hadn't fucked you up for life, you'd be
    able to just reach behind you and grab it!

THERESE MARIE You sonuvabitch! (*Tries to wheel herself
    away.*)

DANNY Where you going, Mom?

THERESE MARIE I'm going to get the elevator man! I'm going
    to get Mr. Collado to wheel me into my bedroom and get
    me into my goddamned bed!

DANNY How're you going to open the front door?

THERESE MARIE I'll wheel myself *through* the front door if I
    have to rather than spend another minute with *you*!

She tries to unlock the wheels of the chair. She fumbles and flusters.

DANNY Mom—

THERESE MARIE Unlock this chair!

DANNY Mom, calm down.

THERESE MARIE Don't you tell me to calm down, don't you
    tell me anything . . . Cruel! Cruel and vicious and mean-
    spirited—and I would have expected it from anyone else
    but you!

Beat.

DANNY You're really unfair, Mom.

THERESE MARIE Yes—and I'm sure you'll tell your therapist *all*
    about it.

DANNY Yeah, Mom—and did it ever occur to you that if you would've just told *any* therapist *anything* about *any* of it, that we might not be where we're at right now?

THERESE MARIE "The wisdom to know the difference," Danny. "God grant me the serenity to accept the things I cannot change—*and the wisdom to know the difference.*"

DANNY Yeah, there's a second stanza to that prayer, Mom— you might've heard of it.

THERESE MARIE I can't change what happened, Danny.

DANNY You know what? This is pointless.

THERESE MARIE Don't you think I would have changed things if I could?

DANNY Okay, Mom, then change *this.* Right now. The doorbell rang—who was it?

THERESE MARIE What does it matter?

DANNY It was a neighbor, right, some neighbor—she came upstairs to your house, and what did she tell you?

THERESE MARIE You're a stubborn mule—

DANNY She told you, "Go fetch your father, he's passed out drunk in the street in front of some bar."

THERESE MARIE On Kearny Avenue. You don't understand the shame back then—the loss of dignity—it was *supper*time, he had just stopped in after work—

DANNY And you went and got him, didn't you?

THERESE MARIE Who wouldn't?

DANNY And you helped him home.

THERESE MARIE The poor man, he was dead on his feet.

DANNY And you carried him up the stairs on your surgically repaired back.

THERESE MARIE I didn't carry him! I had his one arm over my shoulder, I was helping him, trying to bear his weight against the stairwell—it was a two-family house, I couldn't leave him on the porch!

DANNY And when you got almost to the top of the stairwell, Mom—

THERESE MARIE Oh, it was awful—

DANNY Tell me.

THERESE MARIE I felt a crack. And then another crack. And I dragged him to the landing and somehow got him into his bed, and then I crawled into my bedroom, and when I woke up in the morning I was in agony—screaming, crying, I never felt such pain.

DANNY And where were your mother and your sister?

THERESE MARIE Cathleen was at Aunt Dorothy's, I think, and Momma—well, poor Momma, she drank a little too.

DANNY And what happened when you got to the doctor's?

THERESE MARIE Oh, Poppa rushed me to the doctor's, he rushed me, he was beside himself with worry—

DANNY And what did the doctor say?

THERESE MARIE Oh, what does it matter? The surgery was ruined, and that was that. It just happened that way.

DANNY Mom, it didn't just happen that way.

THERESE MARIE What do you want me to say, Danny?

DANNY What do I want you to say?! I want you to say that you got to the doctor and he examined you, and he was at a loss for words, and he wanted to know what the hell happened, and you wouldn't tell him, and you just kept saying, "I don't know," and then he got angry—

THERESE MARIE Oh, he was furious!

DANNY And your father was furious at you too, and he kept telling the doctor, "I told her she was doing too much too soon," because he had been in a fuckin' blackout the night before and had no idea what really happened—

THERESE MARIE Honey, if I had told the truth, it would've killed my father—it would've killed him!

DANNY Right. So instead you kept a secret, and took the blame, and bore the guilt, and spent the next ten years of your life in fuckin' hospital beds in fuckin' East Orange, New Jersey, and spent the next *half century* protecting the memory of a man who didn't fuckin' deserve it, Mom!

THERESE MARIE And if I had blabbed, Danny? What would it have changed? Nothing!

DANNY "Blabbed"?!

THERESE MARIE Even at East Orange General—in the charity ward—he used to come with the books and the assignments. He was convinced I would be better soon and go back to school to become a teacher of the deaf. I couldn't even move—let alone read—but I tried, you know—I didn't think I'd be going to school any time soon, but I tried, you know, I tried.

We see FRANCIS JAMES, *with a stack of textbooks tied in string, talking to an African-American priest,* FATHER LANDER.

FRANCIS JAMES *signs.* FATHER LANDER *speaks and signs.*

FATHER LANDER You mustn't bring the books any longer. It's not fair to her.

FRANCIS JAMES But she's in school, Father. She has to keep up.

FATHER LANDER No. I'm sorry. No. She won't be going back to school.

FRANCIS JAMES Yes she will, Father. You don't know my daughter. My daughter is like me. My daughter has an iron will. She will go back to school.

FATHER LANDER No. She won't be going back. Ever. I'm sorry.

FRANCIS JAMES You don't know my daughter.

FATHER LANDER I do know your daughter. And I love your daughter. Please understand: Your daughter will never walk again. She will never walk. She will never go to school. She may never go home. I'm so sorry to tell you this. But it's the truth.

We see FRANCIS JAMES, *head in hands, stifling heavy sobs.* FATHER LANDER *comforts him.*

Lights down on FRANCIS JAMES.

THERESE MARIE I'll never forget the sound of that. Never ever . . . They thought I'd never walk again. Poor Father Lander. And poor Poppa. He never brought the books again. He never even mentioned it. His dream was that I become a teacher of the deaf. And that dream died that day. Of course I didn't tell him the truth. How could I?

DANNY *pours her a drink.*

DANNY I'm sorry, Mom.

THERESE MARIE (*re: the drink*) Is this my reward? For spilling my guts?

DANNY I don't know what it is, Mom.

THERESE MARIE And if all that hadn't happened? Who knows? I may have never met your father, God rest his soul, and I would never have had you and Justina.

DANNY You were eighteen years old, Mom. I think you deserved to have your twenties. And I think you deserved to have a childhood. And a life free of debilitating pain.

THERESE MARIE One door closes and another door opens. I wouldn't trade the life I've had for the world.

DANNY I'm gonna go get some cigarettes.

THERESE MARIE At this hour?

DANNY I need cigarettes, Mom, what can I say?

THERESE MARIE You mustn't be angry at him, Danny. If you had met him, you would have liked him.

DANNY Mom, if I had met him, I would've kicked his fuckin' ass. And after I kicked his ass, I would've revived him. And when he came to, I would've kicked his ass again 'cuz I don't give a shit if he was Mother fuckin' Teresa— you don't hit a child, you don't beat a child, you don't hit a girl, you don't God-knows-what your own daughter— you just don't do it.

THERESE MARIE It was a different time.

DANNY I don't give a fuck if it was the Ice Age—not on my watch, Mom, no fuckin' way. And not to my mom. Not to anyone. I think your father resented you—

THERESE MARIE My father loved me—

DANNY —He may have loved you, but he resented you. He resented you because you were hearing, and he was intimidated by you because you had your own will of self-determination apart from him. It threatened him. So he kept you down. I'm sorry, Mom—I'm sure he loved you and he was troubled and all that, and he was deaf and frustrated and I even feel sorry for him, but that's what I think.

THERESE MARIE What you think you know wouldn't fill a thimble!

DANNY Okay, Mom. I gotta go.

THERESE MARIE You're wet behind the ears—you need to leave here and go have your own life.

DANNY Sure, Mom—you stayed with your dad till the day he died. You buried your mother, your father, and your aunts before you ever thought of yourself. And I'm supposed to just run off and abandon you—the Little Flower of East Orange—who never did anything to anybody, just so I can go off and have my selfish little life. I love you, Mom. You're my heart. I'm not leaving. That's never gonna happen. Even if it fuckin' kills me!

THERESE MARIE Let me tell you something: I've had a life. A helluva life. A husband, children, friends, loved ones, and thanks to working at TWA, I've seen the world. I've ridden on camels and seen the Sistine Chapel. I went to the Holy Land and the Eiffel Tower, and talked and laughed with people from all over this world. Istanbul, Cairo, Rome, Beirut, Venice, Madrid, Dublin. I gave my heart to the one I loved and was unafraid to do so. Have you done that? Have you seen the sunset over the Dead

Sea? Do you know what it feels like to hold your child in your arms and have him smile at you? To know without hesitation that you'd gladly exchange your own life to save theirs? How many books have you actually read, Danny? How many concerts, plays, galleries? Because I've seen and heard plenty. Plenty. My life was my life. My father was my father—not yours, mine! So if you want to build yourself a cross and hang yourself on it, that's fine. But if you wake up one morning and realize your life is almost over *and you haven't had one*—well, that will be no one else's fault but your own!

DANNY Right. Should I put you to bed or do you wanna stay out here?

THERESE MARIE I don't care what you do.

DANNY Fine. I'll see you later.

DANNY *exits.* THERESE MARIE *looks out at the river.*

DANNY I went to the Dublin House and got ripped till they closed the place. I stopped for cigarettes at the Korean deli on my way home. That's how I ended up here. I have very little memory of what transpired in the deli.

The best I can get at the truth of it is that the deli guy, as I remember it, comported himself toward me in a manner that was utterly and remarkably free of etiquette—and I, in turn, responded to him in a manner completely and enthusiastically free of sanity. Punches flew. I think I took out the plate-glass window. I woke up in a holding cell. Justina wouldn't post bail. Which was prolly a good thing. I pled guilty at trial a couple of months later, got a ninety-day bid, and here I am. It is what it is. Although sometimes I think I let the state of incarceration do for me what I could not do for myself.

Lights up on THERESE MARIE, *sitting by the window, nursing a drink with* JUSTINA.

THERESE MARIE (*midstream*) Oh, honey—it was just gorgeous—gorgeous—like a painting come to life! The sky, different hues of blue as your eyes moved from the horizon to the clouds—oh, and the clouds—perfectly white puffs just loping along lazily amid the rays of sun. It took my breath away.

JUSTINA I'm sure it did.

THERESE MARIE I got off that ferry, and I mean, I had never been there before, no one was meeting me, I didn't know where I was going to stay or even if there was a place for me to stay—and honey, I couldn't have cared less. I was in heaven.

JUSTINA I'm sure you were.

THERESE MARIE It was so beautiful. Just beautiful. Everything I had read about and more. I walked up this gangplank—

JUSTINA Gangplank?

THERESE MARIE You know, like a ramp, from the ferry to the mainland.

JUSTINA It's called a ramp, Mommy.

THERESE MARIE Yes. A ramp. Anyway, there was a concession stand, and I bought an ice cream—one of those frozen custards.

JUSTINA Ummm.

THERESE MARIE And I just carried my little suitcase to this bench and sat down and ate my custard and looked out onto the Atlantic Ocean, and you know, all the tension, the strain, the garbage, it just melted right off of me. The only other time I felt anything like that was the first time I met your father . . . I could feel my neck, and my shoulders, and my back; they all just slowly unkinked themselves and I just sighed . . . And breathed . . . And ate my custard . . . and watched the seagulls . . . for hours. I think it was night before I got off that bench. I felt so happy—so free—I could have stayed there forever. It was almost worth all those years in bed just to have a chance to feel that free. And my father gave that to me. He gave it to me because he knew. Poor man. He knew.

JUSTINA You want some more ginger ale, Mom?

THERESE MARIE What I'd really like is a scotch.

JUSTINA Well, that's not gonna happen because you're taking morphine, so you can kiss that dream goodbye, okay?

THERESE MARIE You know what, honey? I think I'd like to lie down now.

JUSTINA You have to eat first.

THERESE MARIE I'm really not very hungry.

JUSTINA I'm going to go check on the pot roast.

THERESE MARIE Pot roast?

JUSTINA Yeah. Is there something wrong with that?

THERESE MARIE Not at all, honey, it's just, you know, the trick to pot roast is to slow-cook it in its own juices, that's all.

JUSTINA You don't like my pot roast.

THERESE MARIE Honey, I like you. I could give a damn about a pot roast, and really, I'm not very hungry.

JUSTINA You need to eat, Mom. You're not eating.

THERESE MARIE Honey, can we call Danny later? I'd like to say hello.

JUSTINA Uh, I'm not sure if he got a cell phone yet.

THERESE MARIE I'm so glad he decided to take some time for himself.

JUSTINA Yeah, Mom. Me too.

THERESE MARIE You're my honey-girl, Justina.

JUSTINA Yup—and you're my honey-mom, okay? I'll be right back.

She exits. THERESE MARIE *sips some ginger ale. It goes down funny. She stares out at the river. She begins to nod off.*

JUSTINA (*offstage*) . . . Mom?

THERESE MARIE *passes.*

Beat.

DANNY My last act of selflessness was to feel glad that Justina got to be there when she passed instead of me. They needed the time, and I guess me and my mom needed the time apart. Although, in a way, we never were apart and might not ever be. I have no idea what I'm gonna do when I get out. Most of my life I've felt like I was standing on a precipice, waiting for someone to knock me off so that on impact I could miraculously come to my senses and start living like normal human beings are supposed to. But I think the truth is that there is no precipice, and no one could ever knock me off it even if there was one. There is no stopping point. No penalty box for time misspent. No judges scoring for style points. No deluxe accommodations for martyrs, nor barbed-wire fences for the selfish and self-interested. Far from it. The only thing that stops you is death.

Far from an original thought, I'm sure, but it's the thought I'm having. And until death happens? I don't know . . . Except that I firmly believe that grace does not remain invisible to anyone who's looking for it. And even to those who aren't. My mom taught me that. Grace is like your next breath. Until you die, it's always there . . .

A plainclothes detective approaches, cuffs him, leads DANNY *offstage.*

Lights fade.

ACKNOWLEDGMENTS

A play only exists to be staged, acted, and shared with an audience. I get to write because of you. Thanks to everyone who came down to the show. It still feels like a small miracle that people come at all.

Thank you, Oskar, for your love and care and for bringing us home to the Public. Thank you, Phil, for your treasured friendship, sensitivity, and artistic partnership, and your continual willingness to captain my uncertain ships. Thank you to the beautiful, patient, loving, willing, and fiercely talented original cast. Ellen Burstyn: I would call you a miracle were it not for the fact that I got to see just how hard you work. You signed on to a half-written script—that was the miracle! I can never thank you enough. You're an incredible person, and your performance was incredible. To me, you are the simple definition of what an actor should be: Tireless. Humble. Gifted. Giving. Gillian Jacobs: I hope you know how very good you were, and how much you contributed with your fine work and spirit. Sidney Williams: I have no doubt you know how good you were, and I agree with you completely. You're an MVP. Ajay, Howie, and Arthur: You were all leading men in supporting roles, and what a joy—and strong advantage—to have you and to be among you. Thank you so much. Michael Shannon: I don't think I can say enough to actually make you believe how great I thought you were, and how grateful I feel for your hard work, your willingness to dig, and your truly gigantic talent. You're a great actor, you were great in the play, and I'm glad to have made a new friend. SPECIAL THANKS TO GARY JULES FOR THE MUSIC. Last, Dave, Liza, and Liz: What a blessing that we get to choose each other as family and fellow workers for all these years. Onstage and off, there is nothing about you that I do not love completely.

And additionally, much love, respect, and gratitude to the following: the Public Theater and its workers, The LAByrinth Theater Company, Maurice Guirgis, Marie Therese Guirgis, Tala Robinson, Oskar Eustis, Mara Manus, Carole Shorenstein Hays, John Ortiz, John Gould Rubin, John Buzzetti, Elaine Rapp, Maggie Flannigan, Dan Klores, Paige Evans, Marieke Gaboury, Kristina Poe, Veronica R. Bainbridge, Trevor Brown, Chris Rubino, Andrea Ciannavei, Lex Friedman, Brett C. Leonard, Bob Glaudini, Lyssa Mandel, Monique Carboni, Florencia Lozano, Charles Grantham, Laura Ramedei, Nicola Hughes, Mandy Hackett, Jenny Gersten, Jesse Alick, Peter Dean, Brian Roff, Andrew Haring, Mary Carter, Jocelyn Pierce, Kat Glaudini, Danny Naish, Brandon Bart, Danelle Eliav, Narelle Sissons, Mimi O'Donnell, Japhy Weideman, David Van Tieghem, Barry McNabb, Monica Moore, Kat West, Jordan Thaler and Heidi Griffiths, Maggie Burke, Daniel Sunjata, muMs, Yolanda Ross, Darren Frasier, Charles Goforth, Willey Conley, Jeffrey DeMunn, Trevor Long, Stephen McKinley Henderson, Lauren Velez, Michael Lew, Richard Petrocelli, Jessica Kahler, Anne Meara, Eric Bogosian, Lauren Hodges, Aasif Maandvi, Jeffrey A. Horowitz, Kimberly Barswell, Colin Callender, David Deblinger, Michael Filerman, Michael J. Fine, Fred Graver, Ruth Hendel, Susan Kahn, Jackie Judd, Margo Lion, John Markus,

Marianne Mills, Ricardo E. Oquendo, Ira Shreck, Ernie Inzerillo, Sal Inzerillo, Alba Albanese, Dick Benedek, Melissa Palladino, Shane Salerno, Melanie Maras, Kenny Lonergan, Catherine Wadkins, Simone Allmen, Ashley Rae Bonnell, the Kennedy Brothers, Johnny Sanchez, Bennington College, Dina Janis, Frank Vitolo, Joanne Patricia Quinn El-Fayoumy, Dr. Erwin and Susan Kolodny, Tommy Hardy, Jenny Worton, Rupert Goold, Susan Myer Silton, Calvary Hospital, Nicole Depetro, Samir Riad and Alex Riad, KaDee Strickland, Denise Oswald, Jessica Ferri, Joseph Rosswog, Manhattan Theatre Club, Julian Acosta, Carlo Alban, Dave Anzuelo, Vanesa Aspillaga, Stephen Belber, Quincey Tyler Bernstein, Maggie Bofill, Mariana Carreno, Raul Castillo, Andromache Chalfant, Chris Chalk, Rebecca Cohen, Beth Cole, Cusi Cram, Lexi Croucher, Eric DeArmon, Jill DeArmon, Marlene Forte, Yetta Gottesman, Jen Grant, Marco Greco, Daniel Harnett, Mariana Hellmund, Scott Hudson, Laura Hughes, Ron Cephas Jones, Russell G. Jones, David Bar Katz, Jinn S. Kim, Angela Lewis, Padraic Lillis, Father Jim Martin, Adrian Martinez, Chris and Mary Kate McGarry, Tomokoh Miyagi, Megan Mostyn-Brown, Didi O'Connell, Kelly Rae O'Donnell, Wilhemina Olivia-Garcia, Jason Olazabal, Ana Ortiz, Mary Perez, Gary Perez, Gina Paoli, Manny Perez, Portia, Michael Puzzo, Joe Quintero, Elizabeth Rhodes, Elizabeth Rodriguez, Melissa Ross, Al Roffe, Daphne Rubin-Vega, John Patrick Shanley, Alexa Scott-Flaherty, Marshall Sharer, Sarah Sidman, Felix Solis, Ernesto Solo, Phyllis Somerville, Kohl Sudduth, Yul Vasquez, Isiah Whitlock Jr., Kate Whoriskey, Webb Wilcoxen, and especially my mom, Therese Marie Cunningham Guirgis (1925–2006): You gave me everything I needed. I love you.

Printed in the USA
CPSIA information can be obtained
at www.ICGtesting.com
LVHW091135150724
785511LV00001B/167